"IT'S EASY 'SON',
QUIT MAKING THINGS DIFFICULT"

Gerald Hector

Lasting Life Lessons from a Coach and Mentor

WGWPublishing.com

Copyright © 2019 Gerald Hector

All Rights Reserved

ISBN-10: 1-7324781-1-2

ISBN-13: 978-1-7324781-1-4

First Edition

Editing: Lindsey McLaferty, MA

Wandah Gibbs Ed.D.

Cover Art: Mari Smith

Printed in the United States of America

WGW Publishing Inc., Rochester, New York

...This book is dedicated to a Coach, Administrator, Minister, Disciplinarian, Father Figure, Mentor, and Friend. There are few people other than my own father that made such an indelible imprint on my life. I consider them my "kitchen cabinet" of mentors. They have included my parents; Owen and Barbara Hector, Dorothy Cowser Yancy, William H. Gray III, Cornell Leverette Moore, Bishop Claude Richard Alexander, Michael Dean Perry, Roy McClean, and George Thompson.

I've had coaches throughout my life; in my communities, my high schools, and in three different countries, but one individual wove all my early life lessons together and the reality of being a foreigner, into a strategy that benefitted me beyond measure. Everything he taught me has been either confirmed or materialized as I navigate this thing called life.

Coach William P. Moultrie impacted and shaped many lives, and it was always his desire for us all to return the favor to those coming behind us. Howard University was his incubator and track and field was his vehicle of choice in shaping and molding future leaders and social entrepreneurs.

With so much going on within our public discourse today around race, socioeconomic inequalities, and good old fashioned morals, it is my prayer that my feeble attempt at illustrating life through Coach's eyes, will remind us all of simple truths. This great man, the son of sharecroppers, full of wisdom and strength, eventually rose to the highest levels of athletics.

I want to say THANK YOU to a man whose wisdom and insights (crazy as they may sound at times), are needed today more than ever.

Although this book is about my coach, mentor, and friend, I also have to say a special thanks to my wife Sharon-Kaye, and my three children Joshua, Timothy and Kezia for inspiring me to write this book despite the fact that it took me nearly ten years to complete it. I Love you all more than life itself...

Foreward
By
Dr. Rhadi Bullard Ferguson

"No discipline seems pleasant at the time, but painful. Later on, however, it produces a harvest of righteousness and peace for those who have been trained by it."

– Hebrews 12:11 NIV

His words were firm and easily silenced any conversation. Because of the respect we had for Coach, any strong words cut into our flesh, penetrated our souls, and dug into our core.

The initial sting was immediate and I saw it right away. I remember it like it was yesterday. We were in the lower level of the John Harold Burr gymnasium, known affectionally as "The Burr," and Coach Moultrie was verbally leaning into this kid from Jamaica.

I played football, wrestled, and ran track so a quality verbal chaffing was not abnormal for me to witness and experience. When you play football, you develop very tough skin as you get critiqued and reprimanded constantly. Unbeknownst to me at the time, our track coach, William P. Moultrie was a former football coach at Stanford University and at Howard. And boy did I recognize it that day.

On this particular day at track practice, the verbal chastening went from comical to serious in a matter of minutes. I didn't know the backstory of the exchange, nor what had happened to warrant it, but after that day, I knew without a doubt who Gerald Hector was...FOR SURE.

Throughout the years, in spite of this exchange, I watched the relationship between Coach Moultrie and Gerald blossom. It went from Coach/Athlete, to Mentor/Mentee, to a quasi-Father/Son relationship. And I could totally relate because my relationship with Coach had followed the exact same path.

As a world class track and field coach who coached at the Olympics and refereed during the '96 Olympic Games, Coach Moultrie understood the potential in each of his athletes. He knew that some of us would never be world class runners but that we all could be world class people. When he saw that moment in time when we were being or doing anything less than what he believed God had intended for us to do, he would stop us in our tracks.

I, like Coach Moultrie am a Howard University Athletics Hall of Famer. I also had the opportunity to represent the United States at the Olympic Games in 2004 and I too have coached Olympians. I've also coached at the collegiate level and here's what I can tell you: Coaching is tough. It is an art and a science. It requires understanding of when to teach, when to push, when to pull, when to speak, and when to keep silent. But most importantly when it comes to coaching, people need to understand that coaching is a results-driven profession.

And the one thing I remember Coach Moultrie saying constantly was, "It's easy Son.... Just get it done." His approach to life, to track, to academics, to sports, or to whatever task that needed to be handled was one of

NO EXCUSES. He made it his mission to get as many black and brown students in and out of Howard University with a college degree as possible. And if you could win an NCAA championship and become an NCAA All-American along the way, then great. He was driven, he was determined, and he was successful.

I would love to tell you how compassionate Coach Moultrie was, or tell you about the times he inconspicuously dropped a few dollars on the ground to help out a struggling athlete. I would love to tell you about the times I sat in Coach Moultrie's office following graduation as he encouraged me to stay on the path to becoming an Olympic athlete, even though he knew I was struggling. But I will tell you about one story and one story only.

Let me tell you about the time Coach Moultrie almost killed me...I called him while I was pursuing my Master's Degree at Howard University. I was living with my parents who lived next to a golf course. Coach asked me how I was doing and where I was living. I told him, then he asked: "Do you golf?" I replied, "Sometimes but I'm not that good." He replied, "Well, let's go golfing tomorrow at the course by your house." I said, "No problem."

So, Ol' Coach shows up at the house the next morning as agreed, and we head over to the course. We walk into the clubhouse to purchase a round of golf. The man behind the register asks, "Nine holes or 18?" Without hesitation, Coach Moultrie replied, "18--- walking." The man said, "You don't want a cart?" He said, "No, we're going to walk it." Here's where I thought I was going to die.

We had regular golf bags you throw over your shoulder, not the rolling kind you pull along behind you. I said, "Coach, are you sure you don't want a cart?" He said, "Ferguson, it's easy Son, we just gon' get it done." Now mind you...Coach Moultrie was about 70 years old at the time.

For a moment my chest tightened up. Because I was a world class athlete, I tried to play it cool like I was okay with walking the course. For the first five holes, I was good. By hole number 10, my back was hurting. When I got to hole number 14, I was whining and complaining. And that is where I felt I was about to die!

By the 18th hole, I was literally cussing to myself and wondering what in the world I had gotten myself into. Meanwhile, Coach Moultrie was talking away, telling stories, and having a grand ole time. I on the other hand, was MISERABLE!

When we finally completed the course and he took me back to my house, I could not have been happier. I loved seeing him and spending time with him but I felt like that day he snuck in one more workout on me. Knowing what I know now, Coach Moultrie knew how those 18 holes were going to test me and he wanted to see if I could handle it without complaining, whining or talking about my discomfort. I couldn't. And there was a moment between holes 14 and 18 when he said, "Ferguson, if you can't handle this, then you not gon' make it to the Big One Son." He always referred to the Olympics as the "Big One."

Later that evening I replayed what he'd said in my mind over and over and over again. And I told myself, "It's easy. Just get it done." From that day forward I started getting up in the morning and running the entire length of the golf course. I refused to grimace, whine, complain, make faces or show any level of discomfort. Because at the end of the day, nobody wants to hear about the labor pains, they just want to see the baby.

I can tell you right now, without reservation, that out of all the workouts I'd done with Coach Moultrie, the one he put me through on that golf course that day was one of the most powerful ever. It helped me further develop into an athlete and a man. It helped me understand that whining, complaining, and bellyaching are not going to help me complete a task. Staying focused and completing the course is the only way to finish strong. He literally helped me shift my attitude and recognize that nothing is hard nor easy it's just something you've got to do.

I've since gone on to finish my PhD, have two children, a wonderful marriage, went through a tumultuous divorce, and many other challenges. And during all of those milestones, I've had Coach Moultrie's voice in my head coaching me through them and telling me: "It's easy Son. Just get it done."

I was honored when Gerald asked me to write the foreword for his book. As his teammate, fellow alumnus, friend, and someone who also had a special relationship with Coach Moultrie, he knew how much it would mean to me. Coach made us feel as though we were part of his extended family, and I am thankful Gerald is sharing the many lessons Coach blessed us with.

As you go through the pages of this book know that every lesson Gerald got from Coach helped him become the person and man he is today. He is who he is, and I am who I am, and we are who we are, partly because of the many lessons we received at Howard University and from Coach William P. Moultrie.

Enjoy the book and whenever life becomes challenging and you are getting a little bit tired and want to give up, just remember, "It's easy. Just get it done."

Introduction

It's August 6, 2018, Jamaica's 56th day of independence. A good friend of mine has planned a fun-filled weekend of revelry. He's calling it a Summer Playground Fantasy Soiree which will be held in the seaside town of Ocho Rios. From afar, all I can do is imagine the pristine Caribbean waters, the music, the culture, and a long-needed weekend of relaxation and rejuvenation. Imagining is the key word, as I sit so very far away.

As I stir a cup of haterade, my mind wanders off to a faraway place and I find myself reflecting on my uniquely Jamaican childhood. Jonkanoo, Hellshire, and Forum Beaches, fish, festival, bammy, Port Royal, Ocho Rios, Faiths Pen (the original one) - all standard family trips. Jealousy rears its ugly head as I long to partake in the festivities. Life at this moment seems so unfair...

It did not help that I'd started my customary morning devotion by reading from the book of Jeremiah, also known as the weeping prophet. In chapter twenty-nine verse eleven I found these words in the New English translation, "For I know the plans I have for you, says the Lord. They are plans for good and not for disaster, to give you a future and a hope." I found myself asking God why His plans for me that day didn't involve Jamaica. The *badmind* was real in my soul for everyone attending a party or cultural event in sunny Jamaica.

Well after I almost drowned in envy and jealousy, I snapped back to reality, which included making a career decision involving some major risks. To add insult to injury, a young lady smashed my driver's side rearview mirror while driving too close to my vehicle. It is indeed tough, when we realize that life comes at us in all shapes and forms, and most times, unexpectedly. It is in these moments that we give in to the fact that no amount of partying, touring, or longing to have fun can anesthetize us from this thing called life.

I rarely turn on the news these days as I find it depressing. I'm tired of the pontification, grandstanding, and the seemingly irrelevant merry-go-round on which we find ourselves with our political, educational, and religious leaders. We are firmly ensconced in a world where behaviors once thought abhorrent are now commonplace. Politicians seem to be striving to see who can tell the biggest lie (oops I meant embellish the truth), and even when caught with fact-checking, they double down on their statements. Everything seems to be in flux. Or is it? Is it that we need help to figure out the world around us, or is it that this is our new normal? These new norms are so far from the ones I learned growing up. I am not anxious for myself because I am battle scarred in many ways, but I must admit I am anxious about my children's future. How will they navigate these societal changes?

Later, on that same day of August 6th, while watching the news, the most ridiculous question came to mind as I merged my real day with my imaginary one. I asked myself rhetorically, "I wonder if star apples are in season for independence?" What? Where did that thought come from? What does a star apple have to do with anything?

I was born in Jamaica, and spent years around elders who said things that made no sense to me. As a youngster I thought they were super deep in their thoughts, and my little brain could not process such heavy reasoning. "I will get there," I told myself. They were spewing knowledge that I would have to grow up to grasp. When I heard the expression, "*if a nuh suh it guh, sumptm nearly guh suh.*" I've come to realize that such language was other worldly, yet profound. Back in the day, I'd just shake my head and pretended I understood. Was there a fine line or deeper thread to any of these colloquial expressions? And where had the aberrant thought about star apples come from? I was indeed perplexed.

This troubled me for some time. My wife said to me on a number of occasions: "Something has taken your joy. It seems like you have a weight on your shoulders." There I was thinking I was the happy-go-lucky model husband, full of joy and laughter, however my wife, who knows me best, had noticed something was wrong. How could a reference to something I had enjoyed so much as a child have me this perplexed, and what correlation did it have with the news of the day? Did my morning devotions of late, reading Jeremiah, Ezekiel, David, and Hosea about the rebellion of Israel have something to do with it? Good question.

A week or two later things started to make sense. I spoke to a cousin I had not had a conversation with in a while. He sent me a question on Messenger. When I saw his name in my inbox, I instinctively counted the number of years since I'd last seen him. Before college and adulthood stripped away all innocence of youthful vacations, we'd spent every summer together. My parents shipped my siblings and I from Kingston to St. Mary every summer as a way for us to get to know the rest of our family. Today I know better. We were simply sent to Grandma's house for the summer. It was at a distance not easily governed by a quick phone call asking to come and pick us up. Any chance of getting back to Kingston had to be planned well in advance. Major damage to physical bodies would have to occur before my parents came back to get us, and faking an injury to get sympathy was out of the question. It was the perfect set up for their peace and quiet for a good three to four weeks each year. And let me just say that one has not experienced living if you have not found a river basin deep enough for diving, and catching *janga*. Life was good.

We had a simple life in Bailey's Vale, St. Mary; bottle torches for light between the main house and the main road, carrying water in buckets, making rotis on the flat iron tawa, and using the menacing looking outhouse. Despite all of that, it was pure fun because while there we shared the space with well over twenty cousins, aunts, uncles, grandmothers, and great aunts. Family ties were strong. Family was the true incubator that nurtured love and a sense of belonging.

Because we were in the country and had fruit trees on our property, we could climb the trees and pick samples for ourselves. It was the closest thing to heaven from sun up to sun down. We might even skip regular breakfast, lunch, and dinner to gorge on a variety of fruits. We ate guineps, guavas, "coolie plums", June plums, Otaheite (excuse me *eety owty*) apples, mangos for days, and yes that dreaded star apple. That fruit with so much stain in it that our fingers stuck together. That fruit which was either green or purple (my favorite color). My cousins would already have them picked long before we arrived. Come to think of it, I have always wondered when they were in season. I am older now, so I might be mixing up dates, but it flows with the story, so let's keep going.

I felt inexpressible joy while sitting there with my cousins and eating as many star apples as I could until my fingers were glued together and I was *clyde* from overindulging. Parenthetically, we all know that at 10 years of age, the old cliché, "too much of a good thing is not good," does not apply. The star apple was right up there with jackfruit and East Indian mangos as my favorites. This aspect of my visits to St. Mary was nothing short of heavenly. It was a bit rough losing some amenities but being surrounded by so much family made it worthwhile. I felt loved, and we were happy. That was enough.

Unfortunately, one summer as fate would have it, we had to stay in the capital city of Kingston instead. That meant no preponderance of fruit. No going to the river, no *serve mi long*, or policeman button cookies. Kingston was dry, hot, and boring. My family was not wealthy so we did not have a swimming pool or other luxuries that the rich and upper middle class had. It was shaping up to be one of the most boring summers ever.

The only break in the monotony for me on these dreaded summer days in Kingston was to accompany my dad to the tennis courts at the local Public Works facility. He worked in Central Village in the parish of St. Catherine. We lived in Garveymeade, Portmore (a suburb of St. Catherine). He would leave work, and swing by the house to rescue me from boredom before heading out to play tennis. I was too young to *roam street* so going to play tennis with dad was the highlight for at least three days out of the week. It also helped that I had made two friends there, the children of the facility night watchman.

As a youngster, I was a decent tennis player (or so I thought), and I played against the older men who saw it as admirable. I always played on the opposite side from my father. That way, if I hit at least one winning shot, I could talk smack on the ride home. One evening, there were too many adults wanting to play. No young person was going to get onto the courts that night so Watchie, Rude Bwoy and I decided to go exploring the compound to see what mischief we might get into.

While walking around, we stumbled upon a tree I had never paid attention to before. I stared at it intently. I looked at Watchie, then I looked back at the tree. I looked at Rude Bwoy, then back at the tree. My expression said it all. "*A wah kind a tree dis*?' To which they responded in unison, "A one-star apple tree!" I returned my gaze upon the tree, and asked my next question, "*Yuh nuh see di tree a bear*?" To which they replied, "*Long time now. Yuh waan some offa it*?" Grinning from ear to ear and beaming with joy in anticipation, I gazed upon the tree laden with star apples, knowing that the only thing standing between us was time and height.

Now Watchie and Rude Bwoy, being the veterans of the Public Works compound, decided that there were many ways to get at this succulent fruit. In typical Jamaican youth culture, we acquired several broken cinder blocks, and a couple of broken metal chair legs from the office building dump site. We set about to get ourselves some of this fruit. We were armed to the teeth, and ready to gorge ourselves on the bounty we were about to reap. As promptly as we turned the corner and caught sight of the tree, we launched our projectiles. Nothing sounded more pleasing than hearing the pieces of cinder blocks, excuse me, *rockstones*, entering the tree's apex, and the crashing sound of something being hit. With each hurl of a rockstone our anticipation heightened, only to be met with disappointment as no fruit had fallen to the ground. How could this be? All 10-year-old Jamaicans had been primed in the art of flinging. Mangoes would have fallen by now. Guineps would have fallen by now. Why was this tree's fruit so stubborn? I thought of myself as relatively smart, but I was perplexed by our lack of success. We surmised that our rockstones must only be hitting the sides of the fruit, and the velocity must not be fast enough to knock them out of the tree.

In the not so distant future, at just 10 years old I entered Kingston College on my first attempt. I was not short on smarts. I used to be my father's newspaper reader on the way in to work every morning when school was in session. I was pretty sure if I combined my smarts with that of Watchie and Rude Bwoy, we would have great success, despite our demoralizing start. Our final decision was to use the metal legs from the discarded chairs in the dump. We thought that the guillotine effect would bring down the fruit. Watchie was the biggest, but we voted to not let him *fling* our prized weapons because he was *baff hand*, and Rude Bwoy on the other hand had *pretty eyes* that required him to wear glasses. Therefore, the task was left to me and I accepted.

I walked off about 30 paces from the base of the tree, and practiced several mock throws by mimicking the trajectory the weapon would take. The air was thick, and our palpable expectations had me a bit giddy. I leaned back, and set my elbow at a 45-degree angle, then brought the entire arm forward. It was at the top of the extension that I let the metal leg of the chair fly. The turnover rate, the trajectory, and everything was perfect. The turnover coupled with the height, and velocity would surely bring us our just rewards. As it was getting dark, we couldn't see the metal leg of the chair as it entered the canopy of the tree. We simply rushed to the base of the tree to start collecting all that fell to the ground. Our gait and canter from about 30 paces out, would be the envy of Usain Bolt, or Asafa Powell (who was a much better starter). However, disappointment visited us yet again. The only thing we found close to the base of the tree was the metal leg of the chair. Nothing else.

Disappointed yet again, and standing dejected, we heard boisterous laughter echoing from across the parking lot. There sat a Rastafarian man watching us struggle to get some star apples. I wanted to know why he couldn't have helped us get some of the fruit. With a piece of cinder block close by, thoughts ran through my mind in regards to him. Sigh.... After he finished laughing, he stood up and walked over. He was *nice* based on what was hanging from the corner of his mouth. Let's just say it was not a cigarette. He sauntered up to us laughing and in his best English said, "*Is wah unoo a really try do?*" In unison we replied, "We are trying to get a few star apples apiece." In a most innocent and pleading voice I said, "Do you mind assisting us sir?" (Puppy dog eyes and all). He proceeded to tell us, "*Dat is a star apple tree. Dem naw come dung offa dat. Yuh haffi guh up inna di tree and bruck dem off. Dem ting deh will stay up deh an rotten before dem drop off.*" This presented a conundrum because Watchie, Rude Bwoy and myself were all vertically challenged, and this gentleman was too *nice* to climb the tree. Standing there we felt dejected and bewildered.

Needless to say, we did not get any star apples that day, but I had a new-found respect for the tree. I learned later in life that the only way for them to fall from the tree was for them to get so ripened that strong winds could blow them off. Who was going to wait around for them to become that ripe? At that stage, as they fell, they would be smashed. Yuck. I must admit that I was impressed by what the tree stood for in a metaphorical sense. Its resilience and its commitment to staying in place and making people work to enjoy its gifts.

Years later, on this August 6, 2018 day of revelry, the star apple and how many of the issues I was griping about could have been addressed with some good old common sense. If there was ever such a thing as a common sense tree, it would probably have the same characteristics as the star apple tree. We can't just knock down common sense from a tree, instead we have to work for it. In other instances, our cousins, grandparents, mentors, pastors, and spiritual leaders have already picked the fruit for us through experience, training, and hard lessons learned.

Unfortunately, these days, we are going to have to climb up into that common sense tree and pick some fruit for ourselves if we want to survive in today's world. Just like Watchie, Rude Bwoy and myself, not everybody is going to get it, and those that do get it, better use it wisely. You see, common sense tells us that Jamaica's independence occurs once a year. Secondly, the party I was *badminding* is co-hosted by one of my closest friends. So close that he is my daughter's godfather. Common sense implies that I should have planned a vacation trip around the event, putting it in my schedule a year (or even two) in advance. I believe this is the seventh year for this event. But no, I would rather sit in Ithaca, NY and hate on the people having fun.

The star apple comes to mind today on a whole other level. I think we are witnessing people in leadership, and all spheres of life hurling cinder blocks, metal legs to chairs, and possibly a firstborn child to get some common sense from this metaphorical tree. That can be the only explanation the star apple analogy suddenly came to mind while I was watching the news and pining for Jamaica's Independence Day shenanigans. The way things are now, common sense is withering on the vine in the same way that the star apple tree blossoms, bears fruit, then ripens and rots on the stem. It seems that common sense is doing the same today.

As a society and global population, we are reaping the outcome of missed opportunities for picking common sense. Even if we find one or two people lucky enough to get at the metaphorical fruit of common sense, they are sour, bitter, or tasteless because they are not inviting others who might want to share in what they have to offer. Today's leaders for example, though highly educated, seem to lack basic common sense. It lends credence to the expression, "The more education we get, the dumber we become." I am at a loss to come up with any other explanation for what we are experiencing around the globe today. We banter back and forth about this situation in our everyday lives on social media, small gatherings and at the barber shop. However, at this point it seems that all we do is talk about it.

We are destroying the earth's life sustaining natural resources in the name of profit. Some of our fellow citizens are stuck believing that folks from racial backgrounds other than their own are inferior despite the "browning" of the global population. There is a palpable fear that all the things that held moral society together are coming apart at the seams. The sad part is, those who have already partaken in common sense are sitting back and watching while society unravels. We are afraid to apply our common sense because it might bring retribution and unwanted attention. It is easier to simply go along with the flow as long as it does not mess with my tee times at the country club, or erode my time spent in social settings with people who already think and behave as I do. If the people who don't share my views are kept at bay, then all is right with the world...

Switching gears, I would like to introduce you to Coach William P. Moultrie. A man whom I cherished as a coach and father figure. As an adult now looking back on his teachings, I realize he was a visionary with a penchant for navigating life using simple common-sense principles. I've often wondered what he might have said to that 10-year-old boy trying to reach for the star apple. His plain talking, words of wisdom, and common sense are guideposts for me to this day, and I strongly believe they can spark conversations about what we are witnessing today. His words keep ringing in my ears, and I believe it is the simplicity of such wisdom and common sense that we need now more than ever. I spent many hours in his office learning about track and field, but more importantly, about life. I still have questions like, why can't we get at the seemingly obvious issues that plague us individually and corporately? Why can't we get at the star apple of common sense? Why are there no brave souls (myself included) willing to climb that tree of common sense to enjoy the richness and rewards of its offering, but more importantly to share with others?

My hope is that this book answers a question I get asked from time to time by students (especially those of color) who are intrigued by how I navigated from a career in corporate america to one in higher education. It was all in the foundation that was laid for me long before I realized it, enriched by experiences in several settings. You will chart your own course, but I pray that my attempt here gives you a perspective that underscores the fact that we cannot successfully navigate this thing called life without a support system, and folks rooting for us at every turn. You are on that journey now. Enjoy it.

Lastly, let's see if we can figure this thing out together. I promise we won't throw anything at the common sense tree, but maybe we will garner enough collective will to help some of us climb the tree and drop some fruit for the rest of us. Our world needs it. If you don't believe me, turn on your television, peruse online news, or get on social media, and pay close attention to the comments section…

Chapter One

"Son, My Word you Can Take to the Bank"

"Clackety, clack, clack," was the sound ringing in my ears on that sunny summer day. There I was riding the Amtrak from New Haven, Connecticut towards Union Station in Washington DC where I knew no one. For months prior, I had been in conversations with the coach of Howard University's track and field teams. He awarded me a full athletic scholarship.

I'd never met him face to face, but he'd heard about me from coach Leo Brown of Kingston College who had told him of my sporting career in high school, and that I was a good student. Given coach Brown's reputation, the Howard track coach decided to take a chance on me.

I played three sports in high school; football (the original kind), cricket, and track, and I was extremely thankful that my God-given abilities and hard work were about to secure me an education at one of the most prestigious universities in the world. The Mecca, the Capstone, the Black Harvard: Howard University.

There I was months later, looking out the window as the train made its way towards the nation's capital. I could tell I was nervous because there was nothing that passed outside or inside the train that went unnoticed. I had no more nails to bite, and the tissue I held was drenched from my sweaty palms. I guess it is safe to say that I had a healthy sense of nervousness as the train sped down the tracks.

Questions abounded, and I could not relax. What if I don't like him? What if he doesn't like me? Am I too short? Am I too muscular? Am I worthy of this scholarship? What if I mess it up? I had always been confident, and never once had I been intimidated by uncertainty. This was different. Expectations were high, and I didn't have money to attend university anywhere else. In some ways, this felt like a blind date. Though the more I thought about it, it was more like an arranged marriage than a date. Whatever I encountered I would have to live with if I wanted a college degree. It seemed that in each city we stopped along the journey, my questions multiplied, and the ones I considered most difficult to answer got top billing in my mind. The stress was unbearable at times.

When the train finally stopped at the Baltimore Washington Airport station, I knew there was no turning back. Thankfully, a quiet calm came over me. I felt butterflies in my stomach, much like I did right before a track meet, a cricket match, or a football encounter, when a sense of *game time* was upon me. My nervousness gradually turned to strategic thinking. My objective was to meet this coach, do what I know how to do, and get the job done. After all, I am a *Yaad Man an we nuh fraid a nuhbaddy.*

No one greeted me at the station though this was my first time in Washington DC. Union Station in and of itself was an imposing place. Marble floors, vaulted ceilings, and luxury department stores lined the entire station. It looked nothing like the stations I'd seen when I took a train from Kingston to Manchester in Jamaica to my high school soccer camp in that parish. Union Station reminded me of my initial arrival to the United States. Instinctively, I set out to find the taxicab stand. When I left New Haven, my grandmother, aunt, and uncle had given me some emergency money to get me to campus etc.

A natural planner, I had already jotted down the names of the streets along the route from Union Station to the Howard University campus. Doing so was purely a defense mechanism. I figured if while driving I did not recognize street names, I would start asking pointed questions. Anything so the taxi driver wouldn't know this was my first time in the nation's capital, nor that I didn't have a clue where I was going. I am from Jamaica, so that healthy sense of paranoia always keeps me thinking. Some call it street smarts, but I simply call it survival skills.

I jumped into a cab, and stated with confidence, "I am heading to Howard University, and I am somewhat late. Therefore, can you take North Capitol Street as I think there would be less traffic there this time of day?" I had no clue where North Capitol street was, but I wanted to place a stake in the ground that I knew the streets of Washington DC, and that no fleecing of a young impressionable college student would be taking place that day. It was not until much later did I learn that North Capitol Street was one of the fastest routes to campus and only one block away from the taxi depot. To this day, I sometimes wonder if the taxi driver simply humored me. I know if I had been back home in Jamaica, I would surely have heard, "*But dis bredda yah a one eediat.*"

I arrived at Drew Hall on Gresham Street which I would call *home* for the next year. I had nothing with me but a couple of bags and a dream. I soon discovered I was one of only a few freshmen lucky enough to get a single room and I was overjoyed that I did not have to share my room with a stranger. I needed time and space to sort out this new life.

Cellphones were not common then, so I did not know how to get in touch with the coach to let him know I had arrived safely. I pulled out the notes I'd jotted down during our phone calls. I reviewed all the steps he'd told me to take. I had accomplished nine out of ten by the time I got settled into my room.

The tenth step was to meet the coach in the lobby of Drew Hall at 5:30pm. He would come by, pick me up, and take me to the track and field team's interest meeting. My parents instilled in me early on that any time you have a scheduled meeting, you are late if you are not there five minutes before. Therefore, at exactly 5:25pm I was sitting in the lobby of Drew Hall.

In addition to never having met the coach in person, I didn't even have as much as a photo of him. All I had to go on was his distinct voice. His way of speaking often made me wonder if he was a coach or merely a strict disciplinarian. His strict discipline was evident my entire time at Howard, as we held hands and prayed the Lord's prayer after every practice, and after every track and field meet. I knew this much: he always started every teachable moment with the word "Son."

I decided to just sit in the lobby, hoping I'd hear his voice. At exactly 5:30pm I spotted a dark-skinned man with a brisk walk and a confident swagger enter the residence hall. Somehow in that instant I knew it was him. The walk matched the talk, but an even bigger giveaway were his cowboy hat and boots. I had learned he was born and raised in Rockdale, Texas and we all know that "everything is bigger in Texas," including the hats, shoes, homes, cars, and personalities.

Not wanting to embarrass myself by walking up to the wrong person, I sat back and watched him stroll up to the reception desk. Then, I heard that distinctive voice: "Excuse me young lady, has a young man by the name of Gerald Hector checked in yet?" I promise you, I felt as if I was in an old Western, where the sheriff enters the saloon to find out if his suspect has come through. The young lady replied,

"I think so. Is he the one from Jamaica?"

"Yes mam, that should be him. I have never met him in person, but I had his room and everything taken care of ahead of time. I asked him to meet me down here in the lobby at 5:30pm."

"I think that's him sitting over there."

When coach's eyes met mine, I chastised myself; *aren't you going to speak dummy? You know you look kinda weak right about now, why didn't you get up and walk towards him?*

Meanwhile, he simply strolled towards me and said, "Son, are you Gerald Hector?" I replied, "Yes Sir." He said, "It is a pleasure to meet you. Welcome to Howard University. This institution is going to change your life. I am going to say this upfront; we've been talking on the telephone all this time, but at the onset, all I want from you are three things; promise me you will get your degree on time, you will give an honest effort in all you do on the track and in the classroom, and that you will sacrifice the next four years of your life in preparation for the rest of your life."

What was I supposed to say after such an introduction? How are you doing? Or how is your family? How was your ride? Please! None of those pleasantries would've fit. But that was Coach Moultrie for you; caring, firm, and encouraging all at the same time. He was definitely not given to small-talk, however it was during that very first exchange that I received my first star apple.

Unsure of what to say I launched into an endless string of sentences. "Coach, first I would like to take this opportunity to thank you for taking this chance on me, and I will not disappoint you. I will give you 110% every time." Simple and to the point, I matched his directness and wisdom, or so I thought. I should have ended it there, but no, I had to keep on going. "I am impressed that everything you said would be in place when I got here actually was. I know that you must have had something to do with me getting a private room. You also said you'd be here at 5:30pm and you were. That was impressive to me, and I thought I should just mention how thankful I am for everything being taken care of ahead of time." While I stood there wishing I'd kept my mouth shut, he simply responded with:

"Son, my word you can take to the bank. Now let's go to this meeting..."

The star apple I garnered in that exchange was "reliability." That the giving of an honest effort is not something to overlook. Our word is indeed our bond, and folks should be able to take it to the bank. If we show up, we must deliver or move on to something else. However, if you know you cannot deliver in a certain situation, you have options; first, try to improve, second, make an honest assessment of where you find yourself, and third, move on if need be. It makes no sense making promises that you don't deliver.

Coach never once broke his word in my four years while at Howard, though I might have broken mine a time or two during cross-country season. He knew we cheated a bit, but now that I am a little bit wiser, I see why he drove us so hard to reach for nothing but perfection.

Reliability is in the eyes of the person depending on you. Methods of delivery vary however, and I have learned that people address problems differently. If you are being asked to be a square peg in a round hole, then your reliability might take a hit. The three options above present themselves again. Those options are even more relevant when you realize you are not getting any support to address what was discovered. A mentor once told me, "It is better to be somewhere where you are appreciated, versus tolerated." You will blossom in an environment where you and your work are appreciated, and where you're not left guessing if you are simply being tolerated. If those thoughts are in your mind, your reliability will take a hit, because you will then border on simply going through the motions. When that sets in, the last option is best for you. Whenever we feel like we cannot meaningfully make an impact: Why stay just to be a number?

I regularly speak to my friends who own small businesses. Their number one complaint is that they cannot find reliable workers who show up on time, and work a full eight-hour day. Extrapolate that to any sphere of our lives today, and take stock if that is true. At its foundation, being reliable in words, deeds, actions, and outcomes is key. Obviously, it is important that we understand what is expected of us in order to self-assess how reliable we truly are.

I have been blessed over the course of my career to work with some real titans in philanthropic and higher education circles. I have moved around in my career by being handpicked for roles by superiors who furthered my interest in learning, always reminding me to remain humble and teachable. Working for William H. Gray, III and Dorothy Yancy provided me with experiences I wish more young people could have. I would like to think they believed in me because I always delivered for them.

Mr. Gray asked me to be responsible for creating the initial budgets for the $1 billion Gates Millennium Scholars Program. I was surprised and honored at the same time. It was not until after he retired and before he passed away, that he told me that based on our relationship he knew I would get it done in the same way I had delivered on everything else he had tasked me with. He gave me the name "Bad News Gerry" because, while others tended to nuance or sugar coat their responses, I was always willing to tell him the truth about a situation. He told me that my straightforward honesty always played a role in his decision-making. I believe he appreciated that I was not a sycophant. Dr. Yancy recently commented to a colleague in my presence, "One thing about Gerald, nothing will be hidden, and you will know the truth about where you stand at all times." Both Mr. Gray and Dr. Yancy told me that I should never go into a situation without knowing what the possible end is going to be, nor should I go into a meeting without knowing what the possible outcomes might be for my colleagues.

Parenthetically, I later learned that being "Bad News Gerry" was not always a good thing in some people's eyes. Despite it being appreciated by some, in other contexts it was not valued. That made me start to question my successes up to that point. I later realized that it was not me, and recognized instead that not all individuals subscribe to a notion coined by Justice Louis Brandeis: "Sunlight is the greatest antiseptic." Instead, some individuals prefer that the blinds remain closed.

Dorothy Yancy saw something in me, and in my early thirties, she made me her Chief Financial Officer at Johnson C. Smith University. She had seen the reliable and consistent work I did for Mr. Gray, and when he retired, she offered me the job. I still have conversations with her to this day and she continues to guide and advise me. She is always reminding me of what I am capable of, and reminds me of my accomplishments. At times she sounds a lot like Coach Moultrie, "Just go ahead and get it done." Her latest pressure point is for me to get my final degree. She knows I can get it done.

With both Bill Gray and Dorothy Yancy, my reliability was never questioned, but I have learned some tough lessons along the way in terms of making sure that my reliability is never viewed through the lens of other people who have not even taken the time to get to know me. Coach's words are poignant today more than ever, but we must learn to manage the way people tend to create a narrative surrounding our word, our acumen, and our motivation. Our word is all we have and it becomes your calling card regardless of the audience you seek to reach.

Chapter Two

"The Mind Tells the Behind What to Do"

My very first day on campus, I walked over to Burr Gymnasium with Coach Moultrie for our first team meeting of the season. He stopped at his office first. When I entered the room where my teammates were gathering, I could tell everyone was excited to see each other again, which is why they were all there well before Coach showed up. I sat back in my seat and listened to the conversations going on around me. It was that day that I first met Shaun Bell, Gita Bolt, Adae Lemone, Bonnie Simpson, Brian McDaniel, Michelle Felder, Holli Walker, Adrienne Ferguson, and Jevon Williams-who to this day are still my friends.

As we awaited Coach's arrival, having played varsity sports throughout high school, I pretty much knew what to expect from this first meeting. Coach Moultrie would lay out his agenda and expectations for the season. Being at Howard on a full athletic scholarship, I knew that Coach had singlehandedly brought me to the Mecca. So, starting with that very first team gathering, I felt it was my mission to be on my best behavior and to present myself as a model teammate and student.

While we waited for Coach Moultrie, everyone chatted and laughed and shared stories from their summer vacations. But suddenly, the room fell silent. In Jamaica, we explained occurrences like this by saying "An angel is passing through." The room had gotten quiet because Coach Moultrie was approaching. Everyone heard the distinct sound of his cowboy boots hitting the tile floor in the hallway. When he turned the corner into the meeting room, it was the rim of his cowboy that that I saw first.

Coach Moultrie's presence made everyone feel at ease. He cracked a few jokes that, as a freshman on the team, I didn't quite get. Even on that first day, it was evident that everyone on the team loved Coach Moultrie in their own separate and distinct way. Though I soon realized that some days, team members didn't *like* Coach Moultrie because of how hard he pushed us, but everyone certainly respected him and knew he had our best interests at heart.

I expected Coach to give a long, boring talk about the logistics of the season. I thought he'd give us a lecture on practice attendance policy and share clichés like "there's no 'I' in team." But he did none of that. Nope. Coach Moultrie started off the meeting by talking about academics. Right off the bat, he wanted to make it clear that we were at Howard to get an education, and that should be our number one priority.

As he spoke, he looked directly at us freshmen. I found his gaze piercing yet reassuring. While he looked right at me, I heard him say a phrase that I would hear again and again over the next four years: "Son, It's easy. Don't make it difficult."

Coach Moultrie was a big believer in making things as simple as possible. That day, he broke down having a successful four years at Howard into six points. Coach's guide for us was so straightforward and useful, that I not only remember it to this day, I frequently share it with students I meet through my work. I'm paraphrasing, but Coach Moultrie's six points went as follows:

1. You will take 16 credits hours each semester. If you do that, you'll have more than 120 credits at the end of your four years. Those 120 credits will get you a degree, and with that in your back pocket, you'll be able to get on with the rest of your life.

2. Stay away from "dormitory lawyers." Dormitory lawyers are those students you meet who act like experts and tell you which classes are easy A's and which professors are more lenient. Don't listen to anyone who tells you that you won't have to work hard in class or practice. There are no shortcuts.

3. Sacrifice the next four years of your life for the rest of your life. Stay focused and choose a major you'll be able to earn a living on after you leave Howard. Don't waste your time on Basket Weaving 101 or Shoe shining 106 (obviously not real courses but used as a metaphor for selecting challenging majors that have income potential).

4. Academic progress reports will be used as markers to keep you on track. Treat them as such. They are non-negotiable.

5. Give an honest effort at every practice.

6. After graduation, come back to Howard occasionally, and let me know how you're doing in life.

Hearing this list for the first time, I was struck by its simplicity. "That's it?" I whispered to the other freshman sitting next to me. The rules were simple, I would have no trouble keeping them. *This will be a breeze*, I thought to myself.

After sharing this list, Coach Moultrie pivoted from discussing academics to talking about track and field. He rattled off expectation after expectation: Show up for practice every day, tell me if you're injured, don't try to run if you're hurt, be a good accountability partner to your teammates, and keep in mind that the ultimate goal is to make it to the NCAA finals for every event.

It was Coach Moultrie's last expectation however that threw me for a loop. This is when he first broke the news to us freshmen that all of us, even the sprinters, would be running cross-country. When he said this, I looked around at the other freshmen sprinters only to see that we all had the same shocked expression on our faces. I was reminded of Scooby and Shaggy from the Scooby Doo cartoon after they'd seen a ghost or monster of some sort. The upperclassmen, on the other hand, seemed unmoved by this news. They knew the drill.

Having played three sports in high school, I was no stranger to a hard work out. During football season my team had to run for miles at our two a day summer practices. We had to do frequent extra workouts outside of practice, plus weight training. I was accustomed to pushing myself physically, but running cross-country at Howard was something I'd never envisioned. Before coming to D.C., I thought of it as a concrete jungle. Where in the city would we possibly run cross-country?

When Coach asked us freshmen how we felt about the expectation, I didn't dare say anything. But one brave soul said exactly what I was thinking. "Coach," he said. "I'm not sure I can handle running cross-country meets. I've never done that before."

I was surprised that my fellow freshman had the nerve to say this, but Coach Moultrie seemed to expect it. He had an answer ready. "I understand what you're saying, but our season is a long one between the indoor and outdoor meets. You need to get your background work in to be able to run both formats. We must get your endurance and lung capacity up to a certain level. It'll assist you with performance. Those are the basics of track and field. You must get your background in. You'll be able to do it if you believe you can. Let me say this upfront: The mind tells the behind what to do. Look down at my boots and see what they do as I give them commands. Move boot! Stay boot! Go boot!"

This visual display of Coach Moultrie lifting and shifting his boots to simulate the boot moving at his command made the whole team burst out laughing. I joined right along with them. It was funny, though what Coach Moultrie was saying was profound. That's just how Coach always was. He said little things that made us all laugh or baffled us in the moment. But now that I'm older and wiser, I understand why Coach tried to make these interactions so memorable. Because of Coach's little boot dance, I recall this meeting and everything he said clearly. I don't wear cowboy boots like Coach, but I've found myself making this same analogy and shaking my sneakers with my own kids and other teams that I've coached.

The point Coach Moultrie was trying to make was that if we committed our minds to a task, we could get it done and make it happen. Running cross-country may have hurt for those of us who weren't long-distance runners, but the derivative benefits of those workouts served us well when track season came. Of course, Coach Moultrie was right.

Throughout my life, I've found this metaphor to be true time and time again. I experienced it as an athlete and college student, as a professional in corporate America, and now as a university administrator and recent seminary graduate. But this mentality must extend beyond our work life. Take me, for example. I put off writing this book for so long by making up excuses as to why I was too busy or that it just wasn't the right time. But all I had to do was commit to it mentally to get it done.

I believe that most of our victories and losses in life come by way of our mindset and how we process our station in life. At that very first track meeting of my college career, Coach Moultrie handed me a star apple from the tree. He taught me the importance of commitment. When I say commitment, I don't just mean it in the traditional sense. It means committing to spouses, friends, bosses, church, and a bunch of other things, but it also means committing to strive through things that we know will be painful and difficult to navigate.

Even when we know something might be good for us but might cause us pain and turmoil, we usually try to avoid it. If I feel something is too hard or too complicated, I may try to ignore it altogether. Applying it on a corporate level, I think that where the national level is concerned, we can no longer afford to keep avoiding issues. There needs to be a political shift, both in the populous and among our leaders. If you stop and think for a moment, it's easy to identify all the causes society has only half committed to. I believe we need to look at things from Coach's perspective and recommit ourselves to the things we believe are worth doing.

I've always found it a bit comical that year after year, people fall into the same pattern when it comes to New Year's resolutions. With great enthusiasm, people announce their lofty goals for the upcoming year. But, like clockwork, most people fizzle out after about 10 to 15 days of embarking on their resolutions. By the two-week marker, many people let resignation take over. I don't say this to pass judgement, I've fallen prey to this cyclical tradition many times, but it is something I find both fascinating and troubling.

From observations of myself and others, I think I've come to understand the problem with New Year's resolutions: we tend to confuse a vision for change with an idea for change. What's the difference? Ideas come and go, but visions require sacrifice, sometimes painful sacrifice that require we go against our norms and outside of our comfort zones. It's when physical or psychological pain are introduced that many of our resolutions break down.

In my estimation, a vision for change is typically prompted by a crisis requiring change "or else." On the other hand, an idea to change comes about when you believe you have the option to make the change rather than continuing to live as you were. I believe that when we convince ourselves that a change would be nice though not necessary, that's when we tend to fail. It happens when we go through phases where we start projects and quit, or simply commit mentally to our goals without ever acting. We truly are the world's greatest at anything we desire to accomplish, unfortunately that perception is lodged squarely in our minds.

For the sake of analogy, think about the common weight loss resolution. If I want to lose a couple of pounds, I have a few options. I can start a diet, join a gym, or find an accountability partner. The danger in coming up with all these options for change is the temptation to start seeing the end goal as optional. I might think to myself that I'll do a little bit of each, or I'll try one tactic and if I don't like it, I'll try another. If I'm not truly committed to a specific process, I'll likely give up altogether or tell myself that it can wait. Oftentimes, the fits, coupled with the starts, leave us right where we were when we started birthing ideas about change in December. In the short term we might lose some weight, but it returns, and sometimes with added pounds as a reminder.

On the other hand, if I view losing weight as something that isn't optional, I'll have a different approach and ultimately better results. The mind will tell the behind to move, and that it better move if I want to have a long, healthy life. With diabetes, cardiovascular disease, and other ailments on the rise, I'll need a clear vision for change in order to stay in top physical shape. This type of thinking moves us from the realm of a fleeting idea towards a vision that requires sacrifice. With your back against a wall, you're much more likely to commit and stay committed to making a change.

When it comes to creative endeavors, it is all too easy to keep our ideas to ourselves and never bring them to fruition. We hold on to ideas for years without ever committing to the work required to produce what we envisioned. But we will never feel satisfied until we birth that thing that is within us.

Because of my work, I've been around a lot of affluent and accomplished people. I mentioned earlier that they are focused. I've also noticed that most of them have something in common: they are methodical. They remain focused on the task at hand until it is complete, but their methods need to be studied. They suppress doubts. They may think to themselves that they might fail miserably, that they don't have the time, that no one will support them, etc., but ultimately, successful people are able to commit to their visions despite their internal doubts. They don't allow themselves to become their own worst enemy. It is not uncommon to see them talking to themselves. Creativity cannot be harnessed. It needs an outlet. For too many of us, we fight that urge because we want to live within our comfort zone. Books are not written, plays are not produced, and companies are not formed because we talk ourselves out of it.

A lack of commitment can lead to fear and anxiety. The first time I heard Coach Moultrie say "The mind tells the behind what to do" it was a reassuring and motivating concept. But when it came down to competing in a cross-country meet for the first time, the other freshman sprinters and I felt incredibly nervous. There is always a rush of fear and anxiety when we push ourselves to do something new or to venture into uncharted waters. But if we don't work past that nervousness, we'll never know what we are capable of.

When I was a kid, my father took me to see the movie *Jaws*. If you ask Sharon, she'll tell you that to this day, I am an absolute fanatic for Jaws. I've seen it countless times and still watch it every time I come across it on the TV. Sharon has given in to my obsession and simply hands over the remote and heads to bed whenever Jaws is on.

But when I was little, the movie scared me. I was fine immediately after watching it. In fact, I enjoyed the adrenaline rush from watching a scary movie. But two weeks later when my family and I stayed at a hotel on the beach, the movie came back to haunt me. The sound of the waves taunted me. I was young enough to fantasize that somehow, a shark could find its way into the hotel pool. I found myself overwhelmed by illogical thoughts and fear.

At the time, I was taking swimming lessons at the YMCA in Kingston. I knew all the strokes and was comfortable in the water, especially if I stayed toward the shallow end. But at the hotel pool that day, I stood on the deck paralyzed by fear. Eventually, after much persuasion from my father, I got into the water. But I never left the shallow end or took off my goggles, which I usually had no problem doing. I spent the whole time with my head under water looking around for Jaws. The fact that I jumped into the water was a victory because I'd made a commitment to go swimming, and nothing was going to stop me. Now if Jaws was in the water, I would have to figure out a way to get to safety.

When we don't commit, we don't know what we can accomplish. It's always difficult and scary to face the unknown, start on a new endeavor, or challenge existing norms, but sometimes we just have to do it. If not, we'll never become the person we long to be. Now, that doesn't mean we should foolishly jump into something. As an accountant, I always advise people to count the cost first. I believe that eliminating the fear and anxiety that accompanies commitment is achieved through proper, and thoughtful planning. I often share with people this one rule of thumb that my late good friend E. Dean Montgomery once shared with me: "If your outflow is more than your intake then your downfall will be your upkeep and your assets will be in a bind." A simple concept but take a look at what is happening to several once thriving businesses that are now struggling because they ignored this simple concept.

The founders and CEOs of today's mega companies all got to where they are through their tireless work. They had visions, plans, processes, and most importantly, commitment to their ideas and beliefs. Some people may say that these business owners got lucky. They simply had the right timing for the products that made them so wealthy and influential. That may be true, but that doesn't negate the fact that they had to follow through on their own vision. If media reports are accurate, I believe that over time some of these individuals have become corrupt and greedy with power, but I believe their ambition, at its core, is something we can all learn from. They saw what they wanted to accomplish and went after it, even though the long-term outcome has not always turned out to be for everyone's benefit.

It's especially difficult to commit to a vision when it requires revolution. But to achieve real change, we need fearless leaders who commit to their cause and don't back down. What would the world look like today if Martin Luther King Jr. had let fear and anxiety overcome him? Who out there today is willing to fight for what they believe in that same way?

In the upcoming years, the population in the United States will continue to diversify. For example, the higher education industry is a microcosm of what is on the horizon. I believe it will become increasingly important for colleges and universities to catch up and diversify their faculty and staff as well. Administrators need to address this issue head on and truly commit to making changes. This is just one example of how a group of individuals can address a widespread issue. But, unfortunately, this rarely happens. Fear, anxiety, and a whole host of issues keep people from committing to initiatives pertaining to societal change.

As I've mentioned before, people fall into paralysis through analysis or simply don't act because they think someone else will. If we don't wake up and commit to our goals, both as individuals and as a collective, we will stagnate. We will become trapped in the comment section on social media where we feel comfortable enough to complain but aren't challenged enough to act and become a part of the solution.

There's a song I play often by R&B artist K'Jon. The opening lyrics go like this: "Sometimes, it feels like, everything is passing me by. Every now and then, it feels like, my ship has gone and sailed away. But I, I gotta be strong, gotta hold on, it won't be too long."

That song, *On the Ocean*, always strikes a chord with me. It's about hope and staying tough in the face of adversity. The truth is, life can get difficult. But I believe some of the things we face are meant to help us get to the next level in our careers, relationships, and personal goals. But too often, we never get to that next level because we give up too easily. To get out of difficult situations, we simply try to extricate ourselves and let others fight it out.

The Bible tells us that we are not to be conformed to this world. Rather, we must be transformed by the renewing of our minds. The development of new technology in this world is moving at a rapid pace, and we must keep up mentally. But what does that mean? I am an eternal optimist, and I believe that Coach Moultrie was 100 percent correct: The mind tells the behind what to do, both metaphorically and in reality. As I see it, the challenge is that the transformation of the mind is seen as a mystical thing. We often confuse transforming the mind with transforming technology. For example, artificial intelligence is all the rage now and without a doubt it will continue to transform how we interact with time, space, and one another. While this technology is great, we can't allow it to rewrite our identities and fundamentally change who we are.

I believe that in general, most people don't have a true sense of who they are. They cannot see themselves moving in a certain direction. As a collective, I think people of African descent lack a true sense of identity because of the violence and savagery of transatlantic slavery, the Jim Crow era, and other injustices that occurred (and still occur) throughout the diaspora. In effect, we will be pouring the new wines of innovation and progress into old wineskins. Well, we know what the Bible says about that practice. The wine will leak out and become wasted. People of African descent are slowly but surely inching closer to a changed mindset that will in the long run dictate what we tell our "boots" to do. It is inevitable. Technology and deeper understandings of world history, some of which was either hidden or wrongly taught, is coming to light.

The time is now to commit to meaningful change that will benefit everyone in our society, not just a select few. To close the gap of economic disparity, we need to commit to a bold and comprehensive vision. This must happen within the minds of individuals, but also at the city, state, national, and international levels of government. We need to tell these boots to move!!!

I may not be qualified to delve into the specifics of reform, but I adhere to a simple principle that I believe we can learn from: We need to mentally commit ourselves to radical change and follow through with our actions. There are so many pervasive issues we can begin to tackle at a local level. Does your community deal with homelessness? Has the opioid crisis touched individuals in your town? I'm sure the answer is yes. Maybe confronting these issues at a community level is a good place to start.

These may seem like tall orders, but I believe change is possible if we start letting our minds tell our behinds what to do. How can you get started? Turn on the news or pick up your local newspaper. I'm sure something will pop out at you. There is something, some issue within those headlines that needs to be addressed. Could you be the very person to address it? Could I?

Chapter Three

"Son, Henrietta Will Still be There After you Get your Degree"

It was the first week of classes and "The Yard" at Howard University was on and popping. The green grass interspersed with concrete walkways provided a natural flow of student traffic between classes and the Blackburn Center where the cafeteria was located. I was still pretty much fresh off the boat (or train) to be more specific. As a freshman, I did not know a soul from Jamaica. I was clinging to the hope that my newly introduced track and field teammates would be the ones to guide me through this sea of humanity. This rich tapestry of nations. I kept looking around, trying to find the building that housed my first ever college course. Was I to go up the hill, down the hill, across the street, or simply look for the way finders, of which there were none along my path?

I knew that as an accounting major, I should probably make my way to the School of Business, make sure I met with personnel there, and obtain a year by year listing of the courses I would have to take. The buildings all had names attached, but nothing else. That was the first bit of reality. Despite getting a single room in Drew Hall, and the great sense of independence it brought, it finally hit me: I was on my own. No one would be there to wake me up in the mornings, and no one would be pressuring me to study or go to classes. As a student-athlete back home in Jamaica, there was always someone checking in on me. If I was not at a certain place at a certain time, they would hold me accountable. Those days were over. This was college life. Stuff of grown folks.

As I traversed the campus trying to find Fredrick Douglass Hall for my first class with Dr. Medford, I was excited. Although I grew up in Jamaica and was accustomed to seeing brothers and sisters of color, I could not help but gaze upon the beauty of the nations represented on "The Yard." I attended a preparatory school, Our Lady of the Angels, and I also attended an all-boys school at Kingston College. That natural progression was dotted with time spent in Trinidad and Tobago at St. Joseph's College. I had encountered many different cultures, observed the gap in socioeconomic classes, and came across a variety of religious beliefs among my fellow classmates but something was different here at Howard. The weight of the institution settled on my shoulders immediately. Here I was at this storied institution built for "freed men". An institution whose alumni include global movers and shakers, and individuals who fought for freedoms we enjoy today. This palpable sense of purpose all over campus was real. Within a moment however, those high and lofty visions and sensibilities went right out the window as I observed some young ladies walking across "The Yard". "Lawd Have Mercy!" was all I could conjure up. Besides I was only 10 minutes away from the start of my first class, and I was still looking for Douglass Hall.

Things became a little less tense for a moment, when I realized many of the other students I ran into, were just as lost as I was. I had an uncanny knack for running into other freshmen. There I was walking back from Founder's Library and making my way to the flagpole in the center of "The Yard." It was at that time I realized the Lord does indeed answer prayers, and won't He do it every time? I heard someone utter, "*Hey bwoy yuh nah guh a class?*" To which a young man responded, "*yea man, a over inna Douglass Hall mi ago. A mi second to last class fi di day. Wi can link up afta.*" Ahhh, the sweet sound of patois. I felt instantly at ease, and more importantly I would now be able to follow someone to Douglass Hall, while keeping my distance, making sure I did not look suspicious. Once I'd arrived, I could easily ask for directions to the classroom. Now some would ask why didn't you just go into a building and ask an adult where Douglass Hall was? I was a freshman, trying to be cool, and being in control was the name of game. It was not until later in life that I understood a quote that I attribute to musician Quincy Jones, "Ego is overdressed insecurity." It is this same phenomenon that will cause a husband to drive aimlessly looking for somewhere without stopping and asking for directions. I think GPS has probably saved many a marriage!

Less than fifty meters away from the flagpole I'd passed Douglass Hall multiple times. At first, I was relieved, but I realized I had walked past the building at least twice and hadn't even paused to look up at the name on the building. I entered, but this time I dropped the ego, and promptly asked an adult where my classroom was located. I found it with little to no problem, and took a seat. Once inside Douglass Hall, the weight of who the building was named after engulfed me again. I was beginning to soak it all in, but those lofty thoughts were interrupted as I watched my classmates enter the room. Attending Howard University was a true blessing in so many ways.

There I was, sitting in the back of the class wearing my latest Jamaican uptown attire which consisted of a Rastaman belt threaded through the loops of my acid wash jeans, Polo colored shirt, and Travel Fox shoes. Little did I know at the time, but many of us from Jamaica wore the exact same get up. It was like we wore uniforms. Regardless of what people thought, I just knew I was cool. When Dr. Medford entered the classroom, each of us was asked to introduce ourselves, and tell the class where we were from. I heard California, Jamaica, Trinidad, Senegal, St, Kitts, South Carolina, and maybe five or more countries and states. Howard University, The Mecca was already living up to its reputation. We truly were a global representation within the classroom, and I was pleased to know I would be going through this four-year experience with these students.

After my first class, I left through those same doors I'd entered. They led me right back onto The Yard. It was mid-morning, and there were plenty of people sitting out on the grass reading textbooks. I think it was because of the nice weather that a professor had brought his class out onto the grass to conduct his lecture. Out of the corner of my eye, across from the flagpole, I noticed a group of people sitting on a chain link fence that bordered The Yard. The group caught my attention because some of the brothers appeared to have on the same uniform I did. Rastaman belt, Rastaman colored shirts, and the dead giveaway was the Rastaman beret. They looked to be from uptown

Jamaica because of their *cool* complexion, but they obviously had some *rude bwoy* friends. Confirmation was had within seconds when I overheard the wonderful sound of educated patois. "*Yow, unoo a guh over Blackburn? Mi need fi guh si Miss Ansa bout sumpn.*" To which one replied, "*Yea man, mi need fi talk to har as well.*" One thing for certain, no matter how educated we Jamaicans become, our distinctive patois remains. It is uniquely ours.

As much as I wanted to introduce myself to them, I had to make my way to my next class instead. After that I would only have time to get some lunch and return to my room to gather myself for my first full practice. I knew I would see them again. My journey on day one was to make sure I found the buildings where each of my classes would be held for the rest of the semester. As I walked towards each building, I was struck by all the beautiful ladies I saw on campus. I just knew concentration would need to be paramount to make it through these next four years. Although these thoughts were fleeting, I had to catch myself because after all, I was in a long-term (and now long distance) relationship with a Jamaican girl. That was top of mind, so I just observed and kept it moving.

I had a good day. The cafeteria was massive, and the amount of food options we had were mind blowing for a young man whose cafeteria back home offered patty and cocoa bread, sugar bun, bun and cheese, or boxed food of some sort, unless of course we made our way off campus to Ms. Pearl's. Before heading over to North Street, at the smaller campus we had the heavenly half a grotto bread and "bully beef." Those were still good days. Having so many options and possible stations in front of me was a blessing. Howard University was living up to its billing. I was literally in heaven. A couple of hours later it was off to track practice.

As we huddled up for my first ever team practice at Howard University, the seniors joined the group, at which time I met the full squad. It was pretty cool. The first workout however, was much more interesting than I'd thought it would be. We were instructed to run a cross-country course. I was accustomed to building my base with sands, hill training, and such. Now cross-country was the name of the game. Oh well, this is college. This was something new and adjustments would need to be made.

Practice went well and my lungs surprisingly returned to normal after the run. Some of my teammates were obviously cross-country runners, but it was on that first day that I formed a bond with the other sprinters on the team. We were way at the back of the pack, as we made it up the hill to the left of Bishop Caroll High School. I was horrified when an upperclassman declared that we had just completed the short course. That's when I thought I might die, until I heard there were occasions to do a double dip!!!! Two scoops of long-distance running had me believing that I had perhaps bitten off more than I could chew.

The post practice team meeting started after we warmed down and did some stretching. We gathered into a circle then Coach Moultrie came into the room and asked the freshmen how our first day of classes had gone at The Mecca. We each had our favorite stories while we gushed with pride that we were now officially Track Bisons. Playfully everyone laughed at some of the misfortunes that we had suffered while trying to find our classes, and we felt pain for those who were yet to clear the financial aid office. All in all however, it was a jovial atmosphere.

The tone remained good until coach shared with us several key and important facts. He rattled off a few of them, but one stuck with me. It was that day we learned about Henrietta and Big Bubba. Though fictional characters, they were all too real walking across Howard's campus, and they were a large concern for Coach Moultrie where we were concerned. You see, coach had experienced both Henrietta and Big Bubba situations with many of his athletes. He was acutely aware of their corrosive and distractive impact on our potential. The upperclassmen knew who they were, but the freshmen, both men and women were looking at each other, wondering what he was talking about. Here was another metaphor that needed further clarification and insight. I decided right then that I would be heading to see Coach right after practice.

Now, as I look back over my time at Howard under Coach Moultrie's tutelage, I can honestly say that I was a glutton for punishment. I was naïve and in a foreign country, and I needed guidance from an adult who had been through all this before. It became a symbiotic relationship that turned out to be one of the most important of my life. After practice, I casually ventured into his office and sat in one of those famous chairs up against the wall, while Coach made himself comfortable in his big brown leather chair. I began by asking Coach about Henrietta and Big Bubba. Who were they? Were they former athletes? Why did the upperclassmen chuckle as if they knew who they were? Should I be mindful of them coming around? Do you have pictures?

"Son, you will learn during your time here with me that I will do anything to make sure my athletes remain focused on obtaining their degrees. That they are on track with their classes to graduate in four years, and ensure that they sacrifice four years of their lives for the rest of their lives."

He explained that Henrietta and Big Bubba were not real people. They were simply a representation of what can happen when young and impressionable teenagers come to campus and fall in love. Not just any kind of love, head-over-heals kind of love. The kind that makes athletes forget why they are in college in the first place.

"Son, during your time here you will realize that some of the ladies are here to find a husband, and some of the men are here to get a trophy wife. Reject all of that, and put everything in perspective. Each of you is here to get an education. Period. You are an athlete, you are decent looking, muscular, and you are from the islands (the myth is real). You will speak that patois stuff and the ladies will find you intriguing, and Son I can tell you with certainty that if you are doing what you are supposed to do both on the track and in the classroom, Henrietta will find you. If not this year, I can guarantee it will happen several times before you leave this place."

He explained that Henrietta is the type of person who would require most of my time. She would want me close by at all times and would not like to compete with anything or anyone else in my life. He then reminded me of my tight schedule; classes, practice, meets, and all the other necessary obligations required to complete my college experience. He pointed out that I had no time for distractions and that my focus must remain on graduating within four years. "Son, it is quite simple and easy. If you take 16 credit hours per semester, which equates to 32 per year, in four years you will have 128 total credits and you will graduate."

He explained how easy it was but not without stating that if Henrietta entered the picture, I'd find myself taking a minimum of twelve credit hours a semester because of her demands on my time. I'd soon find my track performances falling off because I was always tired. When that happened, I'd find myself under undue stress taking 18 credit hours a semester, while trying to maintain my athletic scholarship. While endeavoring to satisfy Henrietta, before I knew it, my mental sharpness would diminish, and I will have added unnecessary stress to my life. He wanted me to understand that I was supposed to be enjoying the growth and development that college brings instead.

He said that if I sacrificed four years of my life it would impact the rest of my life and in the end, the Henriettas of this world would still be there. If she was gone, then I would easily find another version of her. He then told me, "My job is to warn you before she comes so you can recognize her immediately. Don't get me wrong, you can find a Henrietta while here, but make sure you complement each other. There is a difference. You will know when you see her, because it will make this journey easier not harder. Now get out of my office Son, I got stuff to do."

That conversation with coach really resonated with me. Within less than a month, I became single as my long-distance relationship ended on mutual terms. We were simply too far away from each other to maintain a relationship. However, despite that turn of events I made sure that my Henrietta radar was fully charged and working. Fortunately, there were no Henriettas on the horizon for some time, though a year later, I found my Sharon-Kaye, and thirty plus years later we're still kicking it. After raising three wonderful children we're now happily growing old together, and we are ready to paint the globe red. Coach was right when he explained how priorities matter, and pointed out how easily we can get them mixed up because of emotional decisions we make. The star apple fruit as it relates to Henrietta and Big Bubba was: priority. Lord have mercy, I wish more of this fruit was laying around, or wish there was someone who could regularly go up into the tree like Coach did and pick a few more to share with this world we are currently living in.

I could write a whole book on the topic of priorities. We see the need for it all around us, but have you ever asked yourself why we seem to often miss the mark? Name any aspect of our lives, and you will discover somewhere that our priorities are off track. It might not be glaring, but it is there. Procrastination is the name of the game. Thank God that Sharon keeps me sharp when I am off the reservation.

We have so many distractions today, and with the advent of social media, round-the-clock television, and all the gadgets this world has to offer, we are all regularly challenged with finding the right priorities to pursue. I took Coach Moultrie's advice to heart when he said, the right Henrietta would complement what I am trying to achieve, and not detract me from it. Meeting and marrying Sharon has been the biggest complement to my life in many ways. I am not going to get all mushy and say, "she complements" me, but I will say that being with her made getting through Howard University in four years much easier. She is driven and ambitious, and we have similar goals. She, along with our three children, are my biggest priorities.

Using that logic is not lost on anything else I try to do. The simplicity of Coach's metaphor surrounding Henrietta and Bubba seems silly, but it is pointed. If you think about where we spend our time, talent, and treasure, there is a fundamental question that needs to be asked of our time spent there: Is it making me better or bitter to be doing what I am doing? Is my priority adding to, or detracting from my life? Can it be that simple of an assessment? Yes, it is! We are the ones who keep making things difficult.

Secondly, if our priorities cost us more than we can afford, we might consider reevaluating them. Is it our priority or someone else's? There is an expression I once heard from an old deacon. He said, "Sin will take you further than you want to go, keep you longer than you want to stay, and cost you more than you are willing to pay." If our priorities cause us to be in this box, an immediate red flag should be raised. Nonetheless, with our five senses wired for pleasure, that is sometimes easier said than done.

I have no regrets in this life, because I am a firm believer that my steps are ordered by Almighty God. But if per chance, the 20-year-old Gerald had known what the 40-year-old Gerald knows, I am sure that some of my earlier priorities would have been different. I would not have spent so much time trying to fit into a mold that was not meant for me. I would not have stayed on some of the paths that reduced my productivity, and slowed my growth. We are all masters of our destinies, and it is nobody's responsibility to make us happy. All our priorities need to flow around what it takes for us to survive and live the best life we possibly can.

Chapter Four

"Aww Son, You Have to Practice to Be That Dumb!"

We slowly made our way up the hill from Slowe Hall dormitory and through the LeDroit Park community. As always, we made sure we held our money, clothes, and other belongins close. My teammates and I begrudgingly braved the trek through the darkness of early morning (or very late night, depending on how you look at it). This 5 a.m. expedition was so we could meet the motor coach our team was taking to an indoor track and field meet.

Day trips were the worst. It would take all day to get to that small college in Pennsylvania, compete in the meet, and get back to Howard. We knew we had to go to bed early the night before to get enough rest to compete effectively, but we also knew we had to wake up before 5 a.m. to hit the road.

The getting up part we were sure we could do, but it was the getting to bed on time part that was a challenge. After all, we were college students. Friday night parties with the Caribbean Student Association always thwarted this plan. It was hard getting home at 2 a.m., then getting up at 5 a.m. to catch a bus, then start the meet at 9 a.m. It sounds impossible to me now, but I guess that was just college life. We simply got it done.

When we boarded the bus, I went straight to the back where I had the best chance of catching some uninterrupted sleep. If I was lucky, I could fluff up the carpeted floor and stretch out. Of course, other people talking and getting up to use the bathroom would disturb me, but at least it was something. I had to do what I had to do to make sure I was well rested.

As a team, we had this traveling thing down to a science. We tried to sleep on the way there, compete at the meet, then study on the way back. Couch Moultrie always sat in the first seat on the bus. Even though he sat up front, he heard and understood everything, even whispers. It always seemed like he had bionic ears and eyes in the back of his head.

We stopped at a McDonald's for breakfast, but I wasn't particularly hungry. I just wanted to stay on the bus and sleep. Skipping breakfast would add another half hour of rest, and I wasn't the only one who wanted it. Somehow, I was made the spokesperson to plead our case to Couch Moultrie. I stepped up and approached him. "Coach, a couple of us are not hungry, and we would rather stay on the bus and continue to catch up on some sleep. Is that OK?" His reply was classic. "Son, you need to get that food in your system because I need you to do well on the 4x400 today. You can't do that without fuel, Son. I will see you inside." Needless to say, we got off the bus and ate breakfast.

In typical Howard University fashion, we arrived way before the meet started. That trip wasn't too bad compared to those times where we arrived before the facility even opened and had to wait outside. Coach didn't tolerate being late for anything. By the time the meet started, we were all awake and raring to go. The heat sheets were tracked down and the race assignments were solidified. Teammates exchanged pep talks and gave extra encouragement to the runners close to making NCAA qualifying times.

Getting ready for a day of racing and throwing was a total team effort. This was what we came to the university to do, to compete and pay for our education (or at least in my case.) We came to represent the Mecca and get a world-class education in the process. To us, there was nothing greater than that finish line. This was the unique journey of a Howard University Track Bison; hurdles, obstacles, and countless joyous moments, all wrapped into one four-year experience.

The day passed slowly, but finally it was time for the mile relay race. Coach Moultrie lived for this event. He ate and breathed relays. Even on a bad day, you could see a spark in his eyes when the relays came around. His love for relays took him all the way to the Olympic games, both as a coach and as a referee. We heard all his stories of how he stacked the USA relay team at the 1992 Barcelona Olympics. Coach constantly reminded us of the time a Howard University relay team ran a time of 3:02.66 in Provo, Utah back when our well-known HBCU had only a cinder track. He lived for the relays.

Because Coach Moultrie loved relays so much, we always wanted to compete well for him. And we loved them too. There was just something about being in the thick of things with all that noise and excitement. But the relay was hard. You needed a strategy. You couldn't just go out there and blast everyone out of the water.

It always filled me with anxiety when Coach announced who would run which leg of the relay. He made his decision based on how we trained and even how we performed earlier in the meet. If you weren't on the ball mentally, Coach Moultrie knew it. He didn't hesitate to make adjustments.

At this particular meet, Coach didn't assign me to lead off the 4x400 relay. Instead, he gave me the second leg. But it didn't matter much to me. With Coach Moultrie's relay style, every leg was the dreaded leg. Coach had names for each one. Whoever ran the "Lead Off Leg" had to get out early and get in position. At indoor meets, the staggered starting points were particularly tight spaces. The second runner ran the "Quick Leg" and had to get ahead or at least maintain the team's position. They couldn't let the team slip out of the hunt. The third leg was called the "Power Leg" because the runner had to power down the track and take care of any *dookie*, known as time lost by the first and second runners. Lastly, there was the anchor, the "Clean Up Leg." It was simple: if there were folks in front, the last leg runner had to catch them.

To me, all legs were the same as each one came with its own pressures. Running in a relay was an occasion you had to rise to, period. When Coach assigned me to run the "Quick Leg" in the relay, I thought of my heroes, the Jamaican runners Herb McKinley, Bert Cameron, and USA runner Michael Johnson who at the time was "the man." I tried to channel some of their confidence.

The indoor track at this college had a unique design. It only had three or four lanes and really tight turns. When I ran the open 400 meters earlier in the meet, the turns had been hard to take and I knew it would be even more difficult to maneuver them during the crowded relay. I looked around at the other athletes in the warm-up area and saw some of them talking aloud to themselves. Others looked suspect the way they concentrated so hard. I feared how they'd act in the actual race.

Fifteen minutes later, we lined up on the track, ready to rumble. With a blast of the gun, the race began. My teammate who ran the "Lead Off Leg" had a good start but lagged behind the leaders at the first turn. That wasn't bad, but it forced him to ease into the flow of the pack that ran together.

During the first lap, things tend to look pretty even. But tactically, you can lose ground if you don't take the corners tight enough. That's how Lewis Hamilton did it and upset the Italians in a race I recently watched on the Grand Prix circuit. The turns are where you can gain ground but also where you can lose it. On this track, the turns were as tight as those at the Grand Prix.

Like a lot of indoor tracks, it took two laps to complete 400 meters. I keenly kept an eye on our position. We were still sitting pretty in a tightly bunched group. As the runners made their way down the backstretch, two things came to mind. First, I realized that the changeover zone would be chaotic. Second, I knew I had to figure out how I could show up for my teammate in a way that wouldn't force him to break his stride as he delivered the baton.

As I predicted, the runners started jockeying for position when they got to the final straightaway. The incoming runners all barreled down the track in one big glob of body parts.

It would be impossible to line up in the order they would arrive in. But as the runners got closer, those of us taking the second leg had to start getting in formation and fan out along the passing zone. The goal was to show the previous runner an unimpeded path for the handoff. Thankfully, my teammate picked up on my lead. I led him out of the zone and he successfully passed me the baton.

I took the baton and looked around, noticing the congestion of runners. Thankful that I still had some energy left from my McDonald's breakfast, I felt the adrenaline kick in. It was time to put up or shut up and execute my race plan. From the crowded arena, I heard Coach's distinct Southern Texan accent loud and clear. "Hector! What are you waiting on? You gotta go now, Son!" I kicked it into gear and felt good as I settled into the race pattern.

My moment of clarity didn't last. I started to overthink and then one domino fell after another. My tactics, strategy, and poise all flew out the window. I had a muscular frame and knew I ran with power. I thought I had the lane locked but a competitor got the better of me on the first tight turn. Even if he wore a soaking wet denim suit he would only weigh 125 pounds but he out muscled me to the turn. In my head, there was no way anyone could cut back to the inside so quickly. But somehow, he pulled a Lewis Hamilton on me and I lost my step and had to break my stride.

My next mistake was losing track of the proximity of the others. I could see the two runners in front of me but didn't notice the ones sitting on my shoulders (also known as drafting.) My third and fatal mistake was thinking I could hand off the baton first. Because of my errors, the quick leg collapsed. As a consequence of my mental lapse, I made my final mistake, the nail in the coffin: I ran up into the box. Ahhh, that proverbial box; the place where runners end up behind other competitors, and blocked in by runners on the outside of you.

I heard an audible "OOOHHHH" from my teammates and immediately panicked, worrying about how I would explain my mistake to them: *Well, what had happened was, I thought there was daylight between the runner on the side of the first lane and the infield. I just knew that I could fit through that space, leap-frog into second, then bring the baton around closely behind the first-place runner.* But because I had run into the box none of that mattered. The runners behind me instantly made their move into the top side of the lane behind me. Game over.

I don't recall what happened during the remainder of that race. All I know is that we came in second or third place. After I handed off the baton, I felt the weight of generations of Howard Track and Field runners on my shoulders. I imagined them staring at me from across the globe and down from heaven. I had messed up and I knew it.

For the rest of the meet, I walked around in a fog. I thought my teammates would come and console me. Maybe one of the guys I ate breakfast with that morning or went to the CSA party with the night before would share some words of encouragement. But nope, it didn't happen. I dreaded the team meeting we would have upon our return to campus.

Surprisingly, things seemed to return to normal on the ride home. My teammates and I chuckled it up on the bus, we laughed heartily at dinner, and we swapped stories about what we did right and wrong at the meet. I felt like I was in a good space. But by the time we crossed the Maryland state line, my dread of the team meeting returned. I hadn't crossed paths with Coach Moultrie since the meet ended.

Once we arrived on campus, we grabbed our gear and headed to the Burr Gymnasium. As always, we laughed and talked loudly until Coach walked in and we fell silent. That was the type of respect Coach commanded. A wave of relief came over me as the meeting progressed. We talked through the highs and lows of the meet and who had made qualifying times. Coach made observations about our technique and race patterns and pointed out where we needed to make improvements. Oddly enough, he never mentioned my obvious mistake. I thought he may have forgotten all about it. *Good for me,* I thought. *I'll work on my shortcomings next practice. I'll take this as a teaching moment and move on.*

Coach's legendary meetings could go on forever, sometimes as long as the meets themselves. But for some reason, this one didn't last long at all. Within 20 minutes, Coach dismissed us. Who said there wasn't a God? Thinking I had dodged a bullet, I grabbed my gear and headed out the door alongside my teammates. But then I heard Coach's voice. "Hector, can I see you for a minute?"

As if I were doing the moonwalk, I still faced forward but started to walk backward toward Coach's office. "Yes, Sir," I said as I began what felt like the slowest walk of my life. Every muscle in my legs tensed up as I took each measured step. Somehow, I felt both confidence and concern. I straightened up and made my way to the office.

"You wanted to see me, sir?"

"Have a seat Hector. What happened today in the relay?"

"Nothing much, sir," I replied. "I thought I saw an opportunity to get an advantage on my opponent and I uncharacteristically tried to squeeze by on the inside of the lane."

"Inside of the lane from Lane 1?" Coach asked.

I answered his question with a tinge more confidence, thinking Coach and I were just swapping ideas. "Yes, sir. It was something that I wanted to exploit. I didn't believe the other runner knew how close I was and he was running on the high side of the lane. I saw an opportunity, so I went for it."

"How many lanes were on the track?" Coach Moultrie asked.

"I believe four or five."

"So, what was wrong with going past that youngster in any one of the other three or four lanes?"

His question, hit me like a gut punch. But just as I did while a kid in Jamaica, I channeled my street smarts and tried to see how far I could go in defending my decision. With confidence building, I replied: "I just thought it was best to exploit the weakness. I moved, but unfortunately, my timing was a bit off. I would have used too much energy if I went around the outside."

"Interesting observation," Coach replied. "So, what about all the spikes and other issues that could have happened if you didn't make it by? Did you factor that into your calculations? Did you notice that there were other runners who were also trying to get around you, never mind those who were in front of you? Did you not think they would accelerate as well?"

My confidence took a slight dip because of the rapid succession of questions, but I still replied with some pride. "My calculation drew me to the conclusion that those aspects would be fine because once we got into the straightaway, it would all sort itself out. If my strategy was successful, I would have been out front anyway."

"Awww Son, you have to practice to be that dumb," Coach said without even flinching. "No one thinks like that automatically. You saw a box that would block you in, impede your progress, and put you at risk of being spiked. But yet you still ran right up into it. What sense does that make? I hear what you're saying about the extra energy, but winners always utilize that extra effort. That's what sets them apart. They know they are going to have to put in the work, and they simply do it. Son, it's easy. Quit making things so difficult."

His words humbled me and instantly reminded me why he was the coach and I was the student. There I was, overthinking things and talking in hypotheticals. All I really needed was a good ole' common sense strategy.

That evening, I spent another three hours talking to Coach Moultrie. I racked up hundreds of hours in his office over the course of my four years at Howard. Even after I graduated and started my career, I went there for advice. It was there that I learned many life lessons regarding everything from running, establishing my career, and even marriage. But that night, the star apple I gained from Coach was strategy. Because of the mistake I'd made during the relay that day, Coach taught me a valuable lesson that I still carry with me.

When I was younger, I was reckless and hungry to climb the ladder. Some would say that is laudable, but my eagerness was not always tempered with strategy. Those non-strategic decisions had consequences, and oh boy did I suffer because of a lack of planning. When we are young and think we are smarter than everyone older than we are, experiences and life in general have a way of humbling us. I am a big proponent of the idea that the current generation should surpass the previous one. The things I did not have growing up I wanted. A word to the wise, remain humble and teachable in everything.

The gospel of Luke in the fourteenth chapter and twenty eighth verse records these words, "But don't begin until you count the cost. For who would begin construction of a building without first calculating the cost to see if there is enough money to finish it?" It sounds pretty simple, but given demographic and socioeconomic changes in our society today, some do not have the luxury of counting the cost before attempting something. Even given that scenario, having a strategy is key. "Running up into the box" in living our lives is real, and has its consequences. I had several friends who believed they were going to be millionaires during the Dot.com era. Business plans were drawn up and they dreamed of how they were going to spend their money. Whenever they asked me to look over pro formas, I would ask the question; "So where is the money coming from to pay for the start-up costs?" The looks on their faces said it all. I don't know if I helped them to stay out of the box, or simply told them to go around on the outside by figuring out how to finance their plans.

If you think that launching into something without a strategy is for those of us who are not as smart or sophisticated financially, I would turn your attention to how our governments run on credit, thus mortgaging our children's future. For example, just like during that mile-long relay race, I saw the daylight of an opportunity, and I went for it without a well thought out strategy. It appears some of our governments in the

Caribbean and Africa have also seen opportunities; new roads, bridges, and other infrastructure. The amenities may be beautiful, but the question young people ask is: who is going to repay these crippling loans used to get these amenities?

I have a feeling that we will be spiked, pushed, and tripped as we try to get out of that box, but sitting in it is not an option. We need a strategy, but that star apple is way up at the top of the tree. The younger generation with their technological savvy and deeper understanding of the world's economies, are going to have to climb the common sense tree to pick some strategy. Easier said than done, because our current leaders have been hurling everything at it, yet no fruit is falling. Our global economy is getting more challenged with each passing day.

Developing meaningful strategies forces us to engage with people we currently disagree with. However, we cannot fix what we won't face. I remember in 1996 when Coach Moultrie was invited to Jamaica to discuss the changes in the 1996 NCAA rules. We broke the island into two visits. One session was held at Mico Teachers College in Kingston, and a second was held at Sam Sharpe Teachers College in Montego Bay. The idea was to form a local body that would could advise student athletes and their parents surrounding educational requirements, professional standards, and living in the United States. High school sports have become big business, but even in 2019 we are still seeing many young people coming up short when it comes to preparation. I still have the proposal document gathering dust, but I have not given up on the idea. That strategy still has merit and is sorely needed.

We can look at any issue in our lives both independently and collectively, and see the great need for strategy to bring about success. Our problem remains rooted in our inability to see beyond what our daily subsistence requires. Not truly seeing that what we seek to accomplish individually, can also have a larger effect corporately. There are many smart people in this world. We should not be struggling like this to end some of the ills of this world, but because we lack a comprehensive strategy, we continue to flail in the wind. If you think that is too simplistic an assessment, sit quietly today and ask yourself a question: Is there another way to do this (pick your topic)? Then jot down your responses, and discuss them with a friend. You will be surprised that your thoughts on some of these topics are not unique to you. Extrapolate that across the nations and the world, and then reassess your original thought. It should be revealing just how many simple solutions there are to many of the challenges that plague our world today.

Chapter Five

"Son, Experts are Everywhere But on the Track"

As I sat in the back of the fifteen-seater van, my heart raced with sheer excitement and anticipation. The entire drive from Washington D.C. to Philadelphia, I couldn't sit still, so I was relieved when we finally parked the van. My teammates and I, maybe eight or nine of us, crawled out of the van and started making our way down the crowded streets of Philly.

Once a year, the area surrounding the Franklyn Field stadium in Philly transformed into an entirely different place. As we walked, we bounced along to the sounds of Bob Marley blaring from the speakers. Flags with black, green, and gold lined the streets and vendors walked around selling headbands, wristbands, and t-shirts with the same colors. For a moment, I thought I was back home in Jamaica. I breathed in the unmistakably Jamaican aroma coming from the food trucks; ackee, saltfish, festival, and roasted breadfruit.

It was the Penn Relays that brought us to Philly. Part competition, part carnival, the relay extravaganza, hosted every April by the University of Pennsylvania, was the relays that were the stuff of legends. For runners competing in one of the relays, it was a true rite of passage. For track and field fans in the United States, it was like attending the Super Bowl. (However, any Jamaican would tell you that the Penn Relays pale in comparison to the Boys and Girls Championships back home.) The intense environment of the relays attracts not only track and field fanatics, but coaches eager to recruit their next stars. More importantly, the Penn

Relays bring people from the Caribbean together for annual reunions.

Of course, Coach Moultrie loved the Penn Relays. Like I said before, he lived and breathed any type of relay. My excitement, however, was less for the races and more about just being there, surrounded by my fellow Jamaicans. Additionally, I had to brag at least a little that my alma mater, Kingston College, was the first international school to be invited to the relay carnival. As the pioneers, we opened the floodgates for several Jamaican high schools to participate. I also loved the atmosphere of revelry and fun at the Penn Relays. The friendly rivalry between the United States and Jamaica made it all the more exciting. It was a good day in Philadelphia.

While I wanted to roam around and enjoy the carnival, I had assignments at the meet. Over the course of three days, I had a sprint medley relay, a 4x400 relay, and also had to support my teammates in their races. Business first, party and revelry later. But by Saturday, the third day of the meet, I had time to observe a few races with Coach Moultrie.

A big group of Jamaican fans gathered along the homestretch and Coach wanted to sit right in the thick of things near the finish line. He always talked about how much he loved Jamaican runners, their culture, and their coaches. He once told me the vibe they bring to everything is electrifying. He also had a close relationship with the Jamaican sprinting legend Herb McKinley. When the Penn Relays came around each year, Coach Moultrie wanted to get his fix of the culture.

Back then and to this day, the Penn Relays start of the 4 X 400 heats was a bit of a free-for-all. Because so many high schools (and some colleges) competed, there were no blocks or set lane assignments. Athletes just stepped up and waited for the gun. Once it went off, the runners had to figure out the course for themselves. Over the years, I've seen countless tumbles, dropped batons, and spiking at the relays. But the athletes never seemed to care and neither did I when I was in the mix.

The charged atmosphere at the relays was partially due to the size of the crowd. Seasoned track and field aficionados filled the stands and debated about stats and rankings. They held programs in which they logged times for four days' worth of events. Some years, athletes competing in the Olympics or World Championships ran at the carnival to get an early season workout in the bag. These occasions brought out the most serious track and field fans. The Penn Relays were a big deal.

But in addition to the "professional" fans, the excitement of the carnival also drew in people with a more casual knowledge of the sport. As I learned that day, they had opinions just as strong as the experts. For the first time, I had a window into their observations from the stands. I also had the chance to hear Coach Moultrie's reaction-both to the races, and the behavior of the audience.

Around us, people pretended to take bets on who would win each heat, just like at the racetrack and betting shops in Jamaica. The reward was laughter and exclamations of: *yuh nuh know how fi pick side*. The heats were organized such that schools with slower times ran in one heat and schools with better times ran in another. It came as no surprise that Jamaican high schools had the faster times going into the relays and were therefore all in the latter heats. The Jamaican runners brought with them the intense vibe of the Boys and Girls Championships. As the heat sheet countdown began, you could sense the energy building to a crescendo. Competitors from Kingston College, Jamaica College, Calabar, Wolmers, St. Jago, Camperdown, and St. Elizabeth Technical whipped the crowd into a frenzy. I glanced over at Coach and he looked as giddy as a high school student. He really loved his relays.

As soon as the runners in the more competitive heats took off, the track aficionados in the crowd began their commentary. Those who had recently witnessed the Boys and Girls Championships in Jamaica perused the names of the athletes, the times they achieved in the flat races, their season split times on relays, and what legs they would be running that afternoon. Because I was in the United States at Howard, I had missed the Boys and Girls Championships, so I was happy to hear the fans' perspectives on what had gone down.

At the same time, I was taken aback by the comments made by those less informed about the sport. They based their comments on their observation of the current race or even on the outfits the teams competed in. One comment, the crème de la crème of baseless claims, stood out to me the most when a middle-aged man uttered: *"Da bwoy deh nuh good."*

How could someone say that without knowing anything about the athlete? The commenter clearly didn't follow the local track scene back in Jamaica.

Based off what I heard from others around me, the runner was a promising young man. Back home in Jamaica, we do take schoolboy/schoolgirl sports seriously. The other Jamaican fans in the stands did not seem to appreciate the man's rude comment. One of the track experts pointed out to him that athletes may be nursing injuries and that often times the adrenaline from relay running can cause some surprises. I knew that all too well.

With some measure of balance struck in the argument, I thought to myself how glad I was that someone had corrected the narrative. We could now watch the race in peace. Then, after seeing the youngster run, we could have a better conversation. But a friend of the man who'd made the initial comment couldn't wait to see the outcome before giving her two cents. *"Yuh a eediat. Him neva hurt. Him just nuh good. Look how the track season long and yuh a tell me seh him can't get into shape. Wi inna April boss. Him nuh good. Watch as likkle pressure reach him."*

As she uttered those words, a dead silence descended on our little section of the stadium. Everyone in earshot tried to process what she'd said. Like me, they were shocked by the utter naivete of the statement. The silence didn't last long. You see, in Jamaica, we rarely let people get away with saying stupid stuff like that. We call it out. Based on the year or so that I'd spent in America at the time, I knew that my brothers and sisters in the African American community wouldn't let things like that slide either. I wasn't surprised when another observer chimed in.

"A weh yuh get dat from? Yuh know seh it tek time to recover if di yute was injured. Just siddung and watch di race, and den wi can talk."

With that, laughter spread across the fans sitting around us, just like I expected. I wasn't sure if Coach Moultrie understood the Jamaican patois, so I glanced over at him to see his reaction. Like everyone else, he was fully engaged in a belly laugh. He leaned back while his shoulders moved up and down with each breath accompanying his boisterous laugh. Everything was *irie* again. After all, it was the Penn Relays.

I leaned over towards Coach Moultrie and asked, "Did you hear that conversation? What was that lady and her crew thinking?" Without missing a beat, Coach looked at me and said, "Hector, I thought you knew there are experts everywhere but on the track."
At first, his tidbit of wisdom perplexed me. It reminded me of colloquial expressions elders spoke when I was growing up in Jamaica, things like *"every mickle mek a muckle."* But I knew Coach was getting at something, so I let the comment marinate as I watched the rest of the race.

By the end of the heat, Coach's remark made more sense. I watched the team in question from the lead off to the anchor leg. There was no way in the world the team could have run any faster. The best athlete on the team did what was expected. He impressed me with his form, the cadence of his stride, and his use of energy. Indeed, he was fast. However, two other runners on his team struggled. I had to wonder if they even trained together. Neither of them got out fast enough once they received the baton and their form and cadence needed work. Their speed and turnover couldn't compare with that of their teammate.

When the race ended, I turned to Coach to discuss what we'd witnessed. He was already looking my way. "Son, remember this. The people who do the most talking are the ones who have never experienced anything. They think they know what is happening and what it takes to succeed. They have a cognitive appreciation of what it takes to be great, but they never apply it. They use book knowledge and stuff they see and hear on the news to form their opinions. However, they never live it. They never make up their minds to actually do what they're advocating."

After we arrived back at Howard, I visited Coach Moultrie in his office to talk more about what we witnessed. In typical fashion, I spent about three hours talking to him. The conversation started with small talk about Jamaica, and quickly morphed into a discussion about how a small Caribbean nation like Jamaica could produce so many excellent runners and jumpers-far more than the United States could on a per capita basis.

"Hector," Coach said. "You know what is at the heart of the challenge here? Jealousy. Think about it. I have been to Jamaica before; I've seen what equipment you have. You barely have hurdles at the high schools. You don't have any eight-lane Mondo tracks at the schools. You guys train and run in dirt until you reach the national stadium. I've seen your weight rooms too. We have all this equipment at the high-school level in the United States yet still get our butts whooped. I like the fact that as the supposed underdogs you guys are overachieving."

"Now think about it, that brings jealousy with it. Look at how many coaches lurk around the bull pen and the finish line areas under the tunnels at the Penn Relays. Why do you think they are there? They're in charge of programs that must produce. Jamaica has a product they need. Here in America, football and basketball might attract most of the sprinters and the jumpers. The athletes out of Texas, Florida, and California, the warm-weather states, vie for the top high school sprinters. But there are so many programs in the United States that want to compete. So, we go ahead and recruit some of you and offer you full scholarships knowing there is probably no other way you could afford to attend our schools. That breeds jealousy." These words of insight have stayed with me since. My conversation with Couch Moultrie helped me understand why the fans acted the way they did: subconscious jealousy. The star apple shared on that day was simply gratefulness.

I believe everyone struggles with a tinge of jealousy. We don't always scream our negative thoughts in front of a crowd like the man and woman did at the Penn Relays, but we sometimes feel a sense of envy. "Tell the truth and shame the devil," as my grandma would say. We see folks doing things, and we might say something like; "I wish I could do that." Subconsciously it shows up in us from time to time. It might not be as malicious as the two track fans' banter, but it shows up nonetheless. That is where being grateful can counteract such sensibilities.

Instead of simply being grateful that they were in the presence of these youngsters running, and representing their schools, they had to directly attack the young man. This sounds like a stretch, right? But let me give you an example whereby my wife gave me a different perspective to ponder. She spotted the meta jealousy within me. Follow me on this one.

My middle son Timothy is a very good swimmer. I believe if Sharon and I had bought shares in Exxon Mobil we would be rich given the number of miles we've logged in our Yukon Denali also known as the "swim taxi." I remember one weekend Timothy was scheduled to swim three days straight, with one of the events being a full three-mile long lake swim. As a former athlete, I know about lactic acid build up and the pain it causes. I was genuinely concerned about whether or not my son could swim so much. I registered my concern, and told Timothy that he had to choose which events he wanted to swim in because he couldn't possibly do them all. Timothy was adamant and pushed back saying that he was certain he could swim in all the scheduled events.

After going back and forth, Sharon stepped in on the tail end of our conversation. Timothy was visibly upset and the worst thing you can do is bother any member of Sharon's family. It does not matter who the perpetrator is, if any one in her family is stressed about anything, she is going to resolve it. That day, the father-son relationship did not sway. Her son was perplexed and she wanted to know why.

She asked what was going on, Timothy shared what I had been telling him. Before I could open my mouth to make some finer points, Sharon responded, "Just because you can't do it, doesn't mean that my son can't. That is your issue. If he wants to swim all those races, we will take him to swim those races." When I told Coach this story, he busted out laughing, then said to me, "You married a good one Son." He knew Sharon from when we were dating back in college.

Not only did Timothy swim all the races, he looked like Mr. T because of all the medals he'd won hanging around his neck. I processed Timothy's distress, but more importantly Sharon's words. I did not think it was jealousy at the time, because Timothy is my son; however, I was not as mindful or as grateful as I should have been that I am the father of an athlete who wants to do something exceptional. Sharon may have been onto something, though at the time, as a former athlete myself, I thought I was simply acting as a concerned father. Subconsciously I probably was a bit jealous of the fact that I would not have been able to accomplish what he did that weekend.

We are all gifted differently, and those gifts are from God Almighty. However, when we are around people who are operating in their gifts, we sometimes see them in a different light. We find ourselves comparing and trying to measure up to them. Sometimes we fall short, and the "Imposter Syndrome" kicks in. Rather than being grateful that we have someone who will elevate our focus, we might fall into the trap of simply not enjoying the person's presence and witness of what is possible. It gets worse in a hierarchical structure when the lower level person outshines a higher level one. Gratefulness for the person's talent and influence goes out the window, and comparisons might begin with detrimental consequences.

We can find ourselves on both sides of the coin in this regard. It is something we have to be mindful of each and every day. If I am in supervisory role versus a subordinate role, it does not matter. We have to practice daily to remain grateful for all that is happening around us. Our reactions will dictate how we operate on each respective side of the coin. Being grateful does not come easy, and it is much more common to become competitive. Often times that competition is solely between our ears.

If someone wants to try something different, even if you know he or she cannot accomplish it, support them anyhow. Be happy that there are incredible people around us all the time, and they are going to attempt things that you never thought of. Learn from them, and try not to be that person who sits on the sidelines simply casting negative energy when in fact it is better to be grateful to witness the greatness that might be unfolding before your very eyes.

I used to coach soccer while my three children were playing. I regularly witnessed parents, who were not athletes, but lived vicariously through their children. Some may say that the parents are simply passionate about the game, but I listened carefully to what some of them were actually saying when they were not shouting. Some indicated they wished they could do what their child was doing, thinly veiled as boisterous support. In other words, though I couldn't do it, I am going to will you to do it, but just not better than me. It is the craziest thing to witness, but it should give us pause in our spheres of influence, and remind us all that not everyone will be grateful for what we have accomplished.

Being grateful is also less stressful because the inerrant sense of competition that we might feel is not productive. The older I get, I am grateful just to be alive each and every day, and if I can get to play a round of golf, I am even better. It takes too much effort to constantly be competing with folks, especially when it is all in our minds. Have you ever stressed about what you thought someone was thinking about you, only to find out that the person did not have you on their mind at all? Now calculate how many days you spent worrying about it simply because your competitive spirit was telling you that you were not measuring up. Just a little exercise for you to ponder...

Chapter Six

"Son, They Don't Make Them Like They Used To"

The forecast called for rain, sleet, and snow. From the warmth of my bed, the thought of lining up and running in the predicted weather was unthinkable. I was positive the officials would cancel the meet. Being from Jamaica, I didn't know much about lake effect snow, so I researched it to confirm my suspicions. Hampton University is right on top of a lake, and I figured there is no way on God's green earth they'd make us run outside under such harsh conditions, or so I thought.

All night, my teammates and I waited to hear the good news from the team manager. But Friday night at 11 p.m., there had been no call. Saturday morning at 2 a.m., there was no call. When we finally arose and left for the meet, there was still no call. That meant that at the very least, we would be making the journey to Hampton, Virginia. I boarded the bus and noticed I wasn't the only one praying to the saints to cancel the meet. Nobody had wanted to leave the warm confines of their bed, much less stand outside in the cold for five hours.

But still, no call came. That's just how it is with athletics in the Northeast, or so I was learning. As a freshman from Jamaica, I was about to have a rude awakening to the cruel reality of winter. Thankfully, I had teammates from other Caribbean islands who felt the same way I did. If everyone else on the team could be cool, then so could I. And it wasn't just our team that would be enduring the meet.

As if reading our minds, Coach stood up at the front of the bus to give us a pep talk. "I know those of you from warm climates are wondering if we are going to be running today. I just want to let you know that if the officials decide the meet is still on, we are running. Some of you get nervous when clouds start to form. It's all in your minds. Just put some spit on it and let's go." With that, I added another layer of clothing.

We pulled into the parking lot to find most of the other teams already there. The sky looked deceptively calm outside. The sunshine and the picturesque campus caught our eyes. Nestled beside a lake, Hampton is rather scenic, and we enjoyed the views. (Albeit from the comfort of the bus.) However, we couldn't yet see the elements outside entangling and forming what they call "the hawk." That day, I learned a lesson in weather systems I will never forget. "The hawk" is when low temperatures, water, and wind converge and leave a bitter sting on exposed skin.

"This is good weather," Coach Moultrie said aloud, clearly trying to make light of the situation. "It'll put some hair on your chest." In other words, he was telling us to suck it up and get off the bus. But as the first few of my teammates climbed down the bus steps, their shrieks confirmed my worst suspicions. It was going to be a rough day. My teammates' reactions made the journey towards the front of the bus all the more dreadful. They each exclaimed: "Jesus!" as soon as the outside air hit their skin. I swear, it sounded like we were at an old-time tent revival. "Jesus Christ!" I heard another one of them yell sharply. Either the whole team had caught the Holy Ghost, or it was truly brutal out there.

Bundled up in four layers of clothing, I eventually stepped off the bus. At first, I thought to myself that it wasn't so bad. After all, I was prepared and had dressed appropriately. But this, of course, turned out to be a false sense of security, or, as we say in Jamaica, a *"neva si come si"* moment. As soon as I started toward the stadium, I realized we had gotten off the bus on the leeward side. The lake, however, was on the windward side. As soon as I took a step outside the protective shield of the bus, I too joined in the worship service my teammates were holding. "Jesus Christ!" I yelled and took off running toward the stands.

The cold I could manage, but I had never experienced wind like that before. Every exposed inch of me felt brittle and then went numb. I didn't dare touch my nose or ears because I thought they would break. When my teammates cracked jokes, I feared I would literally laugh my butt off. Somehow, my American teammates from places like New York looked unphased. They were just chilling and trying to convince me that it wasn't so bad. Their nonchalance about the weather tempted me to string together some pieces of cloth from my Jamaican dialect, but I kept quiet for the sake of team spirit.

For the first hour of the meet I sat bundled up in the stands dreading my first event. Soon, I would have to strip back my layers of clothing for warmups. Regardless of the 32-degree weather, I would only be allowed to wear my shorts and vest during the race. With very little motivation to move, I forced myself to make my way down to the track. I reminded myself that I had come to the United States and to Howard to run and that competing in this weather was just a part of the job on the journey towards getting my degree. The cold, wind, and snow were just obstacles I had to conquer.

The team's worship service continued in the stands, and it must have worked because God showed up right on time. Just before my race started, the sun broke through the clouds and added about 10 degrees of warmth. That, my friends, was enough of a win for me. I competed in my flat events under a sunny sky and slightly warmer conditions. By removing my sweats in the heated staging area and warming up properly, I managed my first race just fine. As soon as I had finished, I quickly covered up again and headed back to the stands.

However, as I sat with my team waiting for the last event of the meet, a literal storm was brewing. For once, the weatherman was dead on in his forecast. Something was coming. From the stands, my teammates and I saw it forming over the water. My friends who grew up in the North and had weathered many winters predicted that because the temperature had warmed up a bit, it was going to snow. This puzzled me. I thought it had to be extremely cold for it to snow. In my head, I pictured the large freezers I saw growing up where they kept the heavenly *serve mi longs*. My teammates' comments about the weather seemed counterintuitive but I didn't want to sound uneducated, so I kept my mouth shut.

For the next hour or so, I must have looked like a chameleon. I had one eye focused on the incoming storm and the other on the heat sheet keeping track of the meet's progression. If I were lucky, the storm would hold off just long enough for the relays to finish. But my hopes were dashed in the penultimate hour of the meet.

The storm clouds joined us at the stadium. Some of my teammates will tell you it snowed that day. Others will call the precipitation sleet or hail. Whatever it was, it had caught up to us. Naively, I still had hope they would call off the rest of the meet so we could get back on the bus and go home. The *badmind* started to form inside me as I thought of the bus driver who stayed on the warm bus all day while we sat in the stands exposed to the elements.

As I warmed up for the relay, I felt only a sprinkle of cold rain. The wind had died down, so I felt optimistic. Maybe it wouldn't be so terrible after all. We made it through warms ups and the line up without issue. While I waited for the race to begin, I didn't even think about strategy or what time I wanted to achieve. Survival was my only concern. The other runners around me appeared to feel the same way, making me question why we were even there. Even Couch Moultrie had said just to "keep us in the hunt" for the first leg. Under any other circumstances, I would have balked at such apathy. But on that day, I just wanted to get my leg over with so I could put my sweatpants back on and chill (no pun intended) with the team.

Right before the race started, I felt the butterflies in my stomach. No, it was more than butterflies-it felt like a *John Crow* (what we call turkey vultures back in Jamaica) was trying to spread its wings inside me. To say I was nervous would be an understatement. Of course, just as the race started, all the elements picked up. Wind, snow, and hail hit me as I sprinted. I did

69

everything I had trained to do: I got out early, worked the first turn, and settled into a running pattern once I hit the backstretch. However, no amount of training could have prepared me to run in this weather. Having never experienced such low temperatures before, I didn't know the cold could cause your bodily fluids to stream from your body and freeze. In this instance, it came from my nostrils. Snot streamed across my face and, of course, I couldn't risk breaking my stride by wiping it. I just kept running, hoping anyone watching would understand.

As I ran, I struggled against what felt like an unbearable weight on my back. It felt as though I had furniture strapped to my shoulders. My legs were the ailment. They were so cold and numb that it became difficult to hold my own body weight, or so it seemed at the time. Who knows what was going on? All I know is that somehow, I managed to make my way around the track and hand off the baton.

With my portion of the relay over, I just stood there in shock and complete misery. Only then did I assess my physical condition. I suddenly understood why a few ladies had a disgusted look on their faces as I passed. On closer inspection, I felt the stream of snot that remained frozen all around my mouth and at the top of my lips. But by that point, I didn't even care. I'd just been through hell and back and was happy I'd even made it through. Over the next four years, I would experience many frigid meets, but none of them compared to this first dreadful experience.

With the meet over, my teammates and I hurried to the bus to get warm and head home. The journey to the meet, the fear right before the relay, and the race itself were all behind us. While the day had truly dragged on and the weather almost defeated me, I had completed my events. I don't remember what place we took in the relays, but I do remember feeling pretty accomplished. I, a kid from the tropics of Jamaica, had just survived an entire meet under freezing temperatures and in the bitter lakeside wind. At the end of the day, I had more experience under my belt.

We had a good team meeting when we arrived back at Howard. Our times weren't the best, but we finished the meet without any injuries. Coach Moultrie even said that it was courageous of us to go out there and run under those conditions. But when I thought about it afterward, I didn't understand what was so courageous about competing in the weather. So, the next day, I parked myself in my favorite chair against the wall in Coach's office and asked him what he meant. "Coach," I said. "Why didn't they just call off the meet when the wintry mix picked up? The officials knew people can't run as fast in the cold."

Coach Moultrie held back a laugh and explained how the officials determine whether to cancel a meet. They would never put us in any sort of danger, he said, "It's just a part of competing in the Mid-Eastern Athletic Conference." Coach said I reminded him of David Charlton, an athlete he coached for that famous 3:02.66 4x400 relay in Provo, Utah. Charlton grew up in the Bahamas and every time the clouds rolled in or the temperatures dropped, he would get really concerned about pulling a muscle or not being able to run fast enough. Every time, Coach Moultrie told him the same thing: warm up properly, stretch, and don't take your sweats off until right before the race. Charlton was a "thoroughbred," according to Coach. He didn't know it, but his body was made to perform. Despite his worries, Charlton always got out there and dropped impressive times on any school they competed against, no matter how big the name.

"Son," Coach Moultrie said to me. "What I am trying to say is that having courage in the face of adversity will allow you to experience what you never thought possible. If you're a thoroughbred, you just get it done. Thoroughbreds see obstacles and they figure out ways to get around them. But even before that, they decide not to let whatever scares them or intimidates them keep them from accomplishing what they set out to do. They have ice water in their veins. Son, they just don't make them like they used to."

The next star apple. He taught me the importance of having courage. I left his office reminded that we ourselves govern what we can achieve. Too often, we remain on the plateau of possibilities set by others. To avoid this pitfall in life we need the courage to keep pushing so that we do not settle for a blessing, yet give up on our promise.

I remember back in 2014 when I was writing a white paper concerning the financial challenges Minority Serving Institutions were experiencing, I had to utilize some courage because the "encouragement" (sarcasm) I received from folks who I now realize were not really caring, but rather ungrateful that I would write such a paper. I had just left Johnson C. Smith University to become the Chief Financial Officer for Ithaca College. Even though I had left the Historically

Black Colleges and Universities family, I remained a huge advocate for them. HBCUs are in my very DNA not only because I am a graduate of Howard University and the former Corporate Controller for the United Negro College Fund, Inc before going to Johnson C. Smith University, but I wanted the black excellence that these institutions represent to live on forever.

I was invited to a meeting in Atlanta, GA at one of the hotels at Hartsfield Jackson International airport. I was at a PWI (Predominantly White Institution), and I was not quite sure why I had been invited. I later learned that Bill Gray's nickname for me had gone viral. I was known as someone who will always tell you the truth, and who has integrity surrounding anything I am a part of. I went to the meeting and listened as I was one of the younger persons in the room, and I truly did not have a stake in the discussion. What I heard challenged me because I only heard ideas, not visions focused on the changes that were taking place in the industry. The difference between the two is sacrifice. I was not hearing much about the sacrifices that would have to be made to drive needed change. One young man at the meeting exchanged a knowing glance with me and I had immediately found a kindred spirit in the room as the meeting progressed.

After the meeting, this same young man walked over to me and basically said, "I know you are no longer in the HBCU family, but will you consider writing a white paper on what you see as the key strategies needed for our schools to thrive financially? Oh, and by the way, could you write it having trustees in mind as the target audience?" The paper is now published, but I had to exercise some courage in tackling it because I thought some would be offended as it might be seen as sophomoric or worse. That wasn't the most interesting thing that occurred, I had a couple of people tell me that I needed to be careful when writing such a white paper, or going on the radio to discuss its contents. The concern was that it would hurt my career in the long run. I thought to myself, how does telling the truth hurt your career? Naiveté rules the day.

When all was said and done, the paper actually assisted my career in ways I could never have imagined. The article spawned a regular commentary spot on the HBCU Nation Radio Show. It provided opportunities for me to present at conferences, seminars, board retreats, and board meetings. Because of the paper, I have been introduced to people I have only read about, and travelled in circles I never dreamed I'd be in. What if I had listened to the "dormitory lawyers" who claimed they were concerned about my career? What if, I had lacked the courage to write this thought leadership piece? I have published an update to that paper for an enrollment management association, and I still take calls and questions from other educational leaders on the topic. "Navigating the New Normal: Financial Imperatives for MSI Effectiveness and Avoiding Financial Exigency" is a reality because I took the courage to push past the concerns that could've crippled my efforts.

When we allow others to put us in the box they've imagined for us, it does not benefit us. In the same way that I thought my son Timothy could not swim all those events, there are people out there who will try to limit you. They will put dirt over you, but your courage is all the fertilizer you need in order to blossom.

There is not much more to say about courage. There is no nuance to it. You simply have to step it up and get it done. You have to "put some spit on it," and go. Don't get me wrong, fear is real, but being stuck is much worse. As we look around today, we can pinpoint almost every area of our existence where courage could have brought about change. Business titans and success stories abound. You can read about their early beginnings in garages and bedrooms, and how they grew to be successful. What if they had simply said they were not going to take the necessary risks? What if they'd lacked the courage to step into the unknown?

It not only takes courage to get to the next level, there is also a great amount of courage needed to remain there. There is an old expression: "the higher the monkey climbs, the bigger the target he becomes." Do you have the courage to be "out there" when you know that you might be criticized for your efforts? At times you will be misunderstood and more often than not, have your motives questioned by people who don't even know you. I believe that is what paralyzes us the most. It can cause us to "stay in our place." Well that's when we need ice water in our veins.

Let the precipitation come, you will run right through it. It is when we come out on the other side that we can look back and say: "I did it!" Once that reality sets in, we should then move to see who we might bring along to share in a similar experience. Courage is needed now more than ever, and the world is looking for people who will take up this mantle and carry it.

Like Coach said, "They don't make them like they used to." We can however revisit that observation and create a new and improved version with basic tenets in place. We have the tools to create a firm foundation and we should take on the challenge. Especially for those who want to make a difference in the world. It is not too late to allow common sense discourse back into our daily lives.

Chapter Seven

"Small Juice, Small Man. Big Juice, Big Man"

At the end of my first cross-country meet as a Howard Bison, I collected my lungs, my pride, and my flat running shoes and headed back to the van. This meet, which was held in a tree-lined park on the outskirts of Washington D.C., was my first cross-country competition ever. Suffice it to say, it went a lot differently for me than other sporting events I had participated in.

I wasn't the only freshman who performed less than admirably. The other sprinters in my class looked as bewildered and exhausted as I did, which made me feel a bit better about myself. It also came as a relief that at least one of us, a true long-distance runner, had put on a good show and represented our class well.

Still, I left the meet dissatisfied with how long it took me to run the course. Beforehand I knew I wouldn't stand out or be a major point contributor at the meet, but my pride still took a hit. Let me tell you, it's a horrible feeling when you hit the finish line and look over to see your competitors already back in their sweat suits sitting around drinking Gatorade and laughing up a storm.

To be honest, I was accustomed to winning. I came up in the eighties, the prime era of athletics at Kingston College in Jamaica. My school won almost everything we attempted: football, track and field, basketball, cricket, table tennis, you name it. Back then there was a certain swagger (or, some may call it arrogance) that accompanied anyone wearing the purple and white. I felt unnerved when I got to Howard and fell to some of the competition.

You see track and field was not my favorite sport. I was called up to run a leg on a relay my final year in high school. I was spotted by one of the track coaches while I was playing football earlier in the year. I ran in preparatory school, but for the most part I preferred cricket and football. I got hurt at our annual sports day, and tried to recover from it as quickly as possible because it was also the middle of the cricket season and I was the opening bowler as well. I learned a very pointed lesson that year: In my push to emulate one of my high school heroes, Mabricio Ventura Sr., I wanted to represent my high school in three sports.

Mr. Youngster Goldsmith worked with me to try and get me ready for the Boys Champs as I had a relay leg on the Sprint Medley. My cricket coach and team captain allowed me to explore this opportunity knowing that I would be leaving the following year. I trained with the track team and was feeling good. Running a "dry foot" 49 low or 48 high in dirt was good. That could translate to a 47 high or so on the stadium track. Good enough for a Sprint Medley spot and competing for Kingston College. If I ran a leg on the Sprint Medley relay, that was it! I was good with that. That was back in the 80's. Running such times today would not get you out of the heats.

During a training session I reinjured myself, but this time I told no one, because I selfishly wanted to meet my goal. Forgetting about the team, I kept my injury to myself. Well on the day it counted most, there was nothing there. I ran a most embarrassing leg and let my team down. It happened both in the heats and the finals. I had nothing left to give physically, and I had nothing mentally because my focus was more so on not looking bad. No race pattern, no lift, no push. I let a whole bunch of people down that day. I promised myself I would never ever do that again, but more importantly I would never embarrass myself like that again. I have never talked about this incident until recently, but it has become a teaching moment that I now share regarding leadership, and how the team always comes first. Anyhow, finishing so poorly in this cross-country race simply brought back those memories, as it was only about a year out. The only redemption I felt that year following that horrible event was that our cricket team won the Sunlight Cup later that spring in one of the most epic finals in schoolboy history in my humble opinion.

Still feeling a bit perturbed, I mostly kept to myself on the ride back to campus. But soon, a wave of excitement came over all the upperclassman on the bus. "That's what's up!" I heard someone yell. "Good call Coach!" Curious, I asked a teammate what the big deal was. Apparently, we'd missed cafeteria hours on campus because the meet had gone late. Coach Moultrie had just announced that we'd be going to Mr. Dees for lunch/dinner instead.

Based on the upperclassmen's exuberance, I assumed Mr. Dees was some high-end restaurant where we'd dine like kings. What else would warrant such cheering? I got excited at the thought of a sit-down restaurant experience and a decadent meal.

When the van pulled into the parking lot of the Burr Gymnasium on campus, us freshman exchanged puzzled looks. But the upperclassmen didn't seem the least bit surprised, so we just went along with it. Then, after a few minutes of milling around, Coach herded us in. "Alright," he said. "Let's go over to Mr. Dees and get something to eat, then you can all head back to your rooms, the library, or do whatever else you need to do."

Off we headed to Mr. Dees on foot. Since we were headed to a fancy restaurant, I felt odd carrying my bag full of sweaty clothes and running gear. But my teammates told me not to bother dropping my gear off as we passed close to the dorm. Together, we headed up Gresham Place and over to Georgia Avenue. At the intersection was the world-famous Howard China, the restaurant that would save the day numerous times throughout my college career. That $5.25 shrimp fried rice special was a staple when hunger pangs (white squall) hit after the cafeteria closed for the night.

Further down the street, a bustling corner store caught my eye. Never in my life had I seen a line out the door for a corner store. But as we got closer and the upperclassmen veered in the direction of that same store entrance, I realized what it was. To my surprise, this corner store was our destination: Mr. Dees.

As we waited outside the "restaurant," the front door never shut; a constant flow of customers came in and out. When we finally made it inside, I looked around at the hole-in-the-wall that had made the upperclassmen so excited. It was nothing more than a tiny space with a lunch counter. People walked by with heaping plates of pancakes, bacon, and eggs.

Immediately, I could tell it was a beloved joint with a true sense of community.

The space was so small that the team couldn't fit inside all at once. We had to pile in just a couple at a time to place our orders. As I waited, I observed the upperclassmen pick up their food then open the cooler to grab a bottle of juice. I watched them intently because I subconsciously feared making a mistake even while doing something as simple as ordering food. In Jamaica, we had a name for people who were clearly new to a place or activity: a *neva si come si.*

When it was finally my turn to order and grab a drink, I looked at all the options in the cooler; an assortment of Tropicana apple juice, orange juice, cranberry juice, and a variety of sodas in different sizes, from small cans up to 32-ounce bottles. Not wanting to appear *"wanga gut"* or *"licky licky"* as we say in Jamaica, I grabbed a 16-ounce bottle of apple juice and stepped outside the store.

Coach Moultrie happened to be standing right outside the door talking to a few of my teammates. Not wanting to appear standoffish, I stood close by so I might possibly join in the conversation. I thought to myself that my friends back home would call me *"nuff,"* or nosey, for this, but I felt I had to do what I had to do to become an integral part of this team.

When Couch Moultrie noticed me, he looked down at the bottle of juice in my hand. Had I done something wrong? Should I have gotten a different size juice? Should I have gotten water because juice has too much sugar and was too unhealthy for an athlete?

My teammates who'd been talking to Coach were called inside the store to get their food, leaving me alone with him. "What do you have in your hand there, Hector?" He asked. "Some apple juice, sir," I answered. Without skipping a beat, Coach Moultrie looked at me and said: "Small juice, small man. Big juice, big man." Of course, I had no idea what he meant. All I could muster up in response was "yes, sir." Looking back, that was probably the dumbest answer I could have given.

As always, Coach suddenly turned this conversation about juice into a teaching moment. "Son," he said, "You picking that small bottle of juice tells me a lot about you. You probably picked that small bottle because you didn't want to appear greedy or like you were taking advantage of a situation." He continued, "Let me share something with you. When we left the parking lot, I told all of you we were heading to Mr. Dees and to get whatever you need for dinner. The cafeteria was closed, and I wanted you guys to replenish what you spent running at the meet. That was an open invitation to get what you wanted. Son, I know you can't eat the entire store, which is why I gave an open invitation to get whatever you wanted. I understand your Caribbean cultural norms, but you need to understand something: In this life, when someone has extended an opportunity to you, make sure you maximize it. That person will tell you what the boundaries are in terms of what is acceptable and what is not. Remember that always."

Right then, his number was called to pick up his food, so we didn't have a chance to talk about the matter any further. But that little nugget of wisdom has remained with me to this day. I heard a very similar message from my intermediate accounting professor, Dr. Barron Harvey, the Dean of the School of Business at Howard. A week after our class had taken a quiz and performed quite miserably on it, Professor Harvey came in with a bit of advice: "I am your professor trying to teach you accounting," he said. "you are to use me to get what you need to ensure that you understand the material. You are to use me to learn so you can get out of here, and more importantly-so you can get on with your lives."

Just like Coach Moultrie, Dr. Harvey was trying to get us to take advantage of the opportunities and resources available to us. He wanted us to know that sometimes, it's OK to push the envelope. As people of African descent in the United States, that is something that some people may look down on. But it is most definitely a prerequisite for future success. Over the course of my career, I've found that you can appropriate things in a tactful manner without becoming arrogant or conceited. You can find a balance.

That day at Mr. Dees, Coach Moultrie gave me another star apple. His comments about taking the bigger juice and taking advantage of a situation taught me that bold ambition is a good thing, not a greedy thing.

I've met a lot of powerful people throughout my careers in corporate and higher education. All of them are movers and shakers. Some are arrogant, some humble, and many are somewhere in between. But one thing I've noticed is that almost every single successful person I've met has a laser-like focus when it comes to reaching the goals they've set for themselves.

Successful people are constantly looking for open opportunities and weighing them carefully. On the other hand, the average person sees some new opportunity and doesn't make a move because they prefer the certainty and norms of their current situation. Newsflash: norms don't exist in this ever-changing world. Change is the only constant, and we either adapt or get run over. Most of our challenges (myself included) come from paralysis by analysis. We will analyze an issue to death, when success is realized when we jump. There is only so many times we can count the cost, or review the pro forma of the decision to be taken. We have to execute.

Recently, I shared a quote I saw on Facebook with some friends. It said: "Salary is the bribe you take to forget your dream. No salary earner has ever made the Forbes list." I don't know who said this, but the quote caught my attention, especially because my wife and I had been in the process of talking with our children about their career goals. We've always taught them that they shouldn't limit themselves by thinking they have to work for someone or some company. We encouraged them to look for opportunities to be their own boss as well. Will they follow through? That is up to them at this point. At least we placed that as an option early on. They also see the career paths Sharon and I chose and the sacrifices we made to get there. They have more than enough data to make the right decision that will benefit them.

I have to confess that I have yet to make this leap myself. I keep discussing opportunities, but so far, I've stayed comfortable. But I can't stay still for long. This book is a first "leap" of sorts. I know that I need to keep moving and if I aim low, I will hit it every time. The key for me is: whose target am I focused on? That is for another book, day and time. I will simply ask rhetorically, am I aiming for what the world has conditioned me to shoot for, or is it one that was preordained before the beginning of time? The latter seems to be the right one.

I am not the only one who struggles to see past my comfort zone. I believe that staying within our homogenous groups and hiding within the crowd contributes to this lack of action. Many of us think we are contributing to the betterment of our society when we are stagnant and cowardly. We are yet to scratch the surface, because we are often busy thinking about who will react negatively to what we know needs to be said or done. We might lose friends in the process too. However, if we can get people to realize this complacency, I think we can make a real push toward change. We just have to be willing to disrupt our norms and keep looking for what comes next.

In our current political and social climates, too many people have become apathetic. In my opinion, this apathy is the result of polarization. Some of the policies coming forward in the political sphere are untenable-they are so far on either side of the political spectrum that they can never gain universal approval. In turn, the gridlock makes us feel a sense of hopelessness and helplessness. Everybody is waiting on somebody to do something, and no one does it. I have heard this expression many times over and therefore know it is not a new dynamic for us. Despite knowing we simply can't get past it. The challenge is always who will make the first step.

In a way, this is a self-fulfilling prophecy. We don't get anything done because we don't think we can. Because of our fears, we never set our goals high enough. By setting our sights low, we become prideful and puff out our chests over the small progress that we manage to make even when we know we are called to greater things. There is nothing wrong with celebrating small wins and successes, but the question becomes whether those small wins are along the path we are supposed to take. That little nuance makes a difference in terms of how we should be impacting the world. We set the bar low enough that we can jump over it every time. While standing close to our target goals, it's almost impossible not to hit the bullseye. That way, we get to bask in the glory of our accomplishments each time we hit the mark, while the people who have no voice are looking at us and asking whether we can help them. That puts things in a different perspective.

Unfortunately, our HBCUs are not immune to this dichotomy. They are in dire need of financial assistance that requires action from administrations and alumni. As a community, we have let down our historically black colleges and universities by not giving back to the system. I am guilty of this same issue. I am a graduate of Howard and have been an administrator of two major institutions, but it is easiest to speak to the life changing issues I have experienced. I will not allow negative experiences along the way to prevent me from giving back.

It is our responsibility to secure the legacy of these institutions. Many of us have the means to contribute, but for one reason or another, we hold back. Then, we watch in horror when some of our schools, like Morris Brown, Barber Scotia, and St. Paul's, shutter and close their doors. We feel a sense of loss and frustration when another school is placed on probation or makes its way onto the Department of Education watchlist. But in our frustration, all we do is go on social media to lament. Sure, we have the United Negro College Fund and Thurgood Marshall College Fund, but these organizations can only do so much. It's like an open palm swatting at a major issue. What we need is a greater vision that brings the fingers together to make a fist and knock some of those issues down. This vision will have to be bold. It will require not only a paradigm shift, but enormous sacrifice as well.

Back in 2014, when I wrote the paper on the *new normal* of higher education, questions abounded. Now, five years later, I believe our universities are experiencing the very things I wrote about. I remember being asked if the existing challenges would blow over like other situations had. I did not answer the question, but knew that the real question I was being asked was, "Whether or not we should just wait it out?" When I talked to Couch Moultrie about this, he reminded me that it wasn't the first time I tried to make a change and the idea was not fully embraced. However, I needed to keep trying. In 1996, after taking the trip to Jamaica with Coach to present to student athletes, and meet with local track officials, the results were the same. At the time I suggested creating an oversight body in Jamaica that would act as a liaison between high school sports and the NCAA. "Your ideas were ahead of their time," Coach Moultrie said. "People are not going to listen to you unless there is a crisis. Some people will say you are arrogant, some will say you are silly, but that is what it's going to take. Not just for you-but for those coming behind you." That was the last piece of advice I received from Coach Moultrie. I started writing the white paper in the spring of 2014, and he passed away in July of 2014. Coach always reminded me of an issue I was facing using an example of something we did together or some matter I brought to him. Regardless of the matter, he always required me to be bold, and not worry about what others would think.

When he was back in Rockdale, Texas after his stroke, we often spoke on the telephone. I loved talking to him about Usain Bolt and the rise of Jamaican men sprinting. His words always took on an aura that could be applied to anything. For example, on a political level, why are people of color yet to have the permanent right to vote? Isn't that something people bled and died for to garner. We are in a shifting of the demography of the nation, why are there so many fighting so hard to return to an era long gone? What are they afraid of? Do they believe that what was done to impoverished and destitute nations will also be done to them? Isn't that the craziest thing you've heard? With that backdrop, can you blame them for aiming low? They are going to hit.

Unfortunately, this issue spans almost every sphere. There are churches in similar situations as the one our Historically Black Colleges and Universities are facing. It would seem to me that some church leaders have made politics, influence, and balancing budgets their focus and have lost sight of their purpose: bringing people to a right relationship with God through truth and faith. Our relationship with God now seems transactional. Meanwhile, people around the world are suffering. And it isn't just the Christian church having this issue, it's many of the world's faith communities and organizations. We all have common goals of spreading peace and ending suffering, yet we never seem to make much progress. Where is the ecumenical vision in this age of technology and constant communication that can alleviate the injustices and poverty that we witness across the globe? Are we being bold enough?

Once we get to a place of collective action, then we can begin to tackle world issues. Only then will our ambitions be big enough and bold enough to make a difference. We have to face it-there is no "Messiah" here now to lead us out of the mess we have created. The true Messiah already came and gave us the blueprint, but are we truly following what has been laid out? That is the question. It is on us to clean up what we have done. At some point, we have to stop intellectualizing and theorizing. We need to set goals and adjust to a bold ambition that draws us out of our comfort zones. And to do this, we have to come together. We need to stop settling for the "little juice" when the "big juice" is there for the taking.

Coach Moultrie used to tell me, "It's hard to think big when small has you." I don't know if that is one of his original quotes, but it is a reminder to us all. At first, I didn't understand what he meant, so I pushed back and asked him to elaborate. He explained that throughout his time as a coach, he'd met a lot of young people who were too timid to take what was theirs. Out of fear of what other people would think, they lived below their God-given stationj in life, not wanting to act too bold or presumptuous.

Like me, a lot of people take the small juice from the cooler even when there are bigger and better options available. Coach Moultrie said that he saw this type of fear limit the success of too many students. "To be successful, you can't care anything about what people think or say about you," he said. "Haters are staples in life. But it's your choice to let them make or break you."

Since my days on the track team, I've come to understand a bit more clearly what Coach meant about letting "small" have you. Over the course of my career thus far, I've had to make a lot of big decisions, and they all came at some sort of cost. But most of the time, this cost was more of an exchange. I had to give up what I had gotten comfortable with in order to move on to something better.

Any exchange like this comes with uncertainty. Too often, we falsely believe we're content with what we have and what we've accomplished simply because it is familiar. That is the silly logic we tell ourselves daily. If we don't set our aim too high, we'll still have control. When a new opportunity comes along or we have an idea about how to achieve something, we ignore it because we feel comfortable with what we have in our hands. We don't want to risk putting down what we're holding to pick up something else. To do so, we'd have to let go of our control and security and face the unknown. That is scary.

If we live like this, we pass up on countless possibilities. By holding on so tight to the "small" things in our hands, we don't pick up the bigger ones that may be more enriching and more impactful. We make conscious decisions not to take risks, then we resent those around us who take those leaps and are rewarded with success. When we see our coworkers or competitors getting ahead, many of us tend to experience *badmind*. However, we tend to mask how we really feel by convincing ourselves that we just want to live a simple life. Really? To avoid missed opportunities and the resentment that grows from stagnancy, we need to stop being so tight with what we have. Every now and then, we must stop and think about what we can release in order to make room for more in our lives.

The truth is, people will intellectualize all day long, but when it comes to action, they become paralyzed. Even if someone is on the brink of taking action, they often get the yips. This is when all the "what ifs" take up residence in our mind and if we're not careful, they can shut down our ambition completely. Instead of choosing between what we already have and what we could achieve, sometimes all it takes is a leap of faith. I like the analogy Steve Harvey uses. He says, "You have to jump!!!"

Unfortunately, this type of fear and hesitation also seems to be binding some of today's leaders. I believe that in their hearts, they know how much inequality still exists today. They understand that slavery, Jim Crow, and other atrocities have lasting effects that disadvantage minority groups. However, many can't seem to bring themselves to raise these issues and promote policies that would help level the playing field. Why? They fear the unknown. They would rather play it safe than risk losing the approval of the majority in their district, even though they know taking action is the right thing to do.

Fixing these problems requires bold ambition. It will demand leaders who choose uncertainty over security. The true change makers won't be afraid to cross party lines and negotiate. They will have enough ambition and boldness to reach across the aisle and coalesce around pertinent issues so we can move forward as a nation and world.

This issue reminds me of a situation I lived through in 2015 when the campus I worked at erupted with controversy regarding race, diversity, and inclusion. As the only vice-president of color on campus, I found myself in a unique position. The legitimate issues that students raised became conflated. Soon, it was no longer about race, diversity, and inclusion but rather a vehicle used to make a larger point about a number of long-standing issues they perceived were not being addressed. The boldness needed to tackle the issues that were raised were top of mind for only a moment, and truth be told, some of the folks who had an alternate agenda were not going to step up to address the disturbing issue. Deflection is a good way of putting it.

This leads me to a final point about ambition as we try to choose the right size juice. Our ambition must be based in empathy, and we must pursue our ambitions in such a way that it invites others to see things from new perspectives. I've been black all my life. My race and the color of my skin have shaped my experiences in obvious ways. I grew up in a majority black country, I came to the United States and studied at Howard. I worked for the United Negro College Fund, and I was a Chief Financial Officer at an HBCU for almost a decade. But after taking a detour for six and a half years, I am back in the HBCU family again at Morehouse College. These environments impacted and continue to impact the way I see and experience the world. To make change and to convince others to join in my efforts, I need to understand that other people don't share these same experiences. They don't understand the realities of inequality and injustice. To put it more bluntly, being called a n----- or having a 9mm Glock pointed in your face by a police officer who thought you were stealing your friend's equipment after playing music at your own event will remind you of the difference between the theory of equality and the reality some of us live in.

To change the status-quo, others need to arrive at a place where they are willing to relate to another person's experiences and imagine what it's like to walk in another person's shoes. That requires a "big juice" versus a "small juice" mentality meaning you are willing to do whatever is necessary to see the change and you are reaching for higher heights. This is painful, but until we get to that point, some folks will never leave their comfort zone and make a true impact. When someone never experiences racism or hatred, they believe it no longer exists. Without the proper perspective, people will continue to hold on to what they believe in order to maintain their status, sanity, and mistakenly clear conscience.

Chapter Eight

"You Can't Ask a Quarter Horse to Run a Derby"

It is well known among the students at the Howard business school that by your junior year, your classes will be kicking you in the rear. Introductory courses and general education requirements are over. It's time to dive in deep to your specific major. And mine, accounting, was the most difficult. One spring semester, I took Intermediate Accounting II. Let's just say taking this class coupled with spring indoor and outdoor track seasons was brutal. However, there was no way to avoid going this route if I wanted this degree, and graduate within four years.

As a junior, I was really starting to feel the pressure. I had to keep my grades up at all costs. It wouldn't be long before I'd have to start applying for internships and post-graduate positions. Being a good student and athlete was becoming increasingly difficult. At times, even sleep seemed to be a luxury.

I remember feeling particularly crushed after taking an exam. I'd pulled an all-nighter to study but still felt perplexed while taking the test. When I caught up with my classmates afterward, we couldn't help but laugh when we realized none of us had come up with the same answers. Walking out of the exam, I heard several people say they wanted to give up the accounting major altogether. My poor performance on that test put me in a funk for the rest of the day. I showed up for track practice out of sorts and tired. What made it worse was that I had missed lunch.

At practice, we were working on block starts. Now, the team had a bit of a rivalry when it comes to this and I'll admit that I was far from the best on the team. I could hold my own, but I had teammates who were much better at it than I was. I tended to pop up out of the blocks, but since I didn't compete in the 100 meters, I was never too bothered by it.

At that practice, Coach Moultrie seemed to be focusing on me. I could tell he was bothered because he kept yelling out to me and repeating my name several times before stating the point he was trying to make. After such a tiring day, Coach harping on my starts really got on my nerves. Each time he said my name it sounded like fingernails being dragged across a chalkboard. I tried my best to keep my cool, to ignore my anger, and to fix what I was doing wrong. Shaun Bell even tried to help me out, reminding me that I needed to stay low for longer. But no matter what I did, I just couldn't get it right that day. It was a rough day and focusing was not in the cards.

On my next attempt, I botched my start yet again. Clearly, Coach Moultrie who was unhappy, yelled: "Hector, Hector, Hector! Why are you making this so difficult, Son? It's easy. Quit making it so hard." When he said that, something in me snapped. It was as if I was a gun and Coach Moultrie had pulled the trigger with his reminders. Without stopping to think, I went off.

"Hey, wait a minute!" I said. "I'm trying my best. I've had a rough day and I didn't get much sleep last night. I'm just a little off today."

What I said may not have been that bad, but my tone was beyond disrespectful. It was filled with anger, and everyone on the team detected it. I heard an "oooohhhh" erupt amongst my teammates and Shaun looked over at me, clearly wondering if I'd lost my mind. Suddenly, things started moving in slow motion. I could hear my teammates' footsteps but couldn't tell if they were moving toward me to comfort me or moving away from me to hide from the pending consequences of my outburst.

As soon as the shock of what I'd done wore off, I started envisioning the worst-case scenario. What would I do without my track scholarship? I had no other way to pay for school. My mind started to move a mile a minute trying to find a way out of the hole I had just dug myself into. Finally, Coach Moultrie responded to my outburst. Without a break in the cadence of his tone, he simply said: "Son, I want you to get back down in those blocks and do as I say. If you aren't going to listen to me, at least watch your teammates who are coming out of the blocks correctly."

All I could muster up in response was, "yes sir." Then, I swallowed loud enough that it could be heard across Georgia Avenue. As practice went on, I kept quiet. My teammates still looked stunned by what had transpired. They all knew me as a reserved person, some may have even taken my kindness for weakness. But not that day. That day, my whole team saw the *yaad man* in me come out, Jamaican accent and all!

In the locker room after practice, I asked my teammates for prayers. Coach hadn't called me to his office, but I had decided I needed to go to him and apologize in person. I knew better than to disrespect my elders. I wasn't raised that way, and I've never done so again in any professional setting. Sharon often reminds our children (me as well when I am off track) to, "own your stuff," and I try to live by that principle. We're all responsible for how we react to life's situations and the words we choose to respond with.

From the locker room, I headed straight to Coach's office. When I arrived, I was surprised to see Coach Moultrie in good spirits. He smiled and welcomed me in. A few of my teammates were also in his office, so for about an hour and a half we just shared casual conversation. While I waited for what seemed like an eternity to talk to Coach alone, I considered just leaving. But I knew if I did, my own grandmother Edna Mae Broderick would descend from Heaven herself and snatch me by the neck. Speaking with him was the right thing to do.

Once everyone else left the office, I launched right into my apology. "Coach, I just wanted to stop by and apologize for my outburst today," I said. "That was so uncharacteristic of me that I have to admit I'm a bit ashamed. I was having a bad day in classes and I was tired. I should have acted more responsibly, and I am sorry."

"Son," he said. "I'm glad you came to apologize; it is the right thing to do. At practice, I saw a side of you that I knew was there all along. Your response today simply came out of frustration because you just weren't getting it. That's fine. I understand that. To be honest, I was pressuring you hard today because I wanted to see how you would respond. You're a junior now and a de facto leader on the team, but still, neither myself nor your teammates can seem to read you. But your outburst today showed me that you have a little fire in your belly. You want to do things right and your response to pressure showed me you are truly passionate and have real emotions. That is what I wanted to see, Son. Thanks for sharing."

As Coach Moultrie spoke, I sat there totally confused and not fully understanding what he was trying to tell me until much later in life. To be a good leader, you must have a fine balance of empathy, sympathy, and care, all the while being forceful when necessary. You must show emotions every now and again so others can relate to you. At the time, however, I was baffled that Coach was impressed by my outburst instead of being angry.

After our brief conversation about the day's drama, Coach and I segued into a typical conversation about track and field. There was always something to discuss with Coach; he was a repository for all things track and football. Compared to Coach, I was far from an expert when it came to track, so he usually steered the conversation. But as I was thinking of discussion points to bring to the table, I remembered a race that happened over the summer. I'd been meaning to talk with him about it for some time now, but kept forgetting. The race I'm referring to was the 4x400 at the 1991 World Championships. It had been a total upset and I wanted to get Coach's take on what happened.

On the American team was Andrew Valmon, Quincy Watts, Danny Everett, and Antonio Pettigrew.

(Pettigrew was that year's champion in the 400 meters.) The US quartet was the clear fan favorite and had an impressive season behind them. Everyone expected them to win. But in the end, they were beaten by the quartet from Great Britain comprised of Roger Black, Derek Redmond, John Regis, and Kriss Akabussi. When they won, I along with everyone one else, was surprised beyond belief.

"What did you think of the 4x400 at the World Championships?" I asked Coach. Of course, he had a long explanation for what he believed the American team had done wrong and what the British team had done right. I don't remember everything Coach said, but the conversation went on for at least an hour. And I learned quite a bit by listening.

"Kriss Akabussi ran a textbook leg," Coach Moultrie said. "He got out and sat right on Antonio's shoulder then outkicked him down the straight. He ran it smart."

In response, I said something about the fact that Akabussi had been a hurdler before he was drafted to run the anchor leg in the 4x400.

"Hector, let me tell you this," he responded. "There are two things you need to know about track and field. Number one, you must know the difference between a thoroughbred and a donkey. Number two, you can't ask a quarter horse to run a derby. You see, Akabussi is a thoroughbred. He went out there and he flat out got it done. Hopefully, the USA team will adjust and be better next year."

Like so many times before, I looked back at Coach Moultrie, with a confused look on my face. What on earth was he talking about? The next day, I decided to go research the breeds Coach had mentioned to try and figure out the point of the metaphor. I knew what a donkey was, of course. They move much slower than thoroughbred horses, so that part of Coach's analogy was clear. What I didn't know was the difference between a thoroughbred and a quarter horse. From what I gathered, I learned that when it comes to racing, both types of horses are trained with different expectations.

Thoroughbreds are trained for longer races, such as a derby. Some are even used in show jumping. They perform the best in races longer than a mile. Think about triple crown winner Secretariat---he was a thoroughbred. On the other hand, quarter horses compete best at the quarter mile. While thoroughbreds tend to be lean and sleek, quarter horses are usually stocky and muscular.

The more I read about both types of horses, the better I understood the point Coach Moultrie was trying to make in his metaphor. We are all unique individuals who have unique purposes, wills, and goals. We may find people who are like us and share our opinions, but they are never exactly like us and they will go on to accomplish different things.

This is true, but I took away an even more important lesson from my conversation with Coach coupled with my brief research on both breeds of horses. Olympic medal winner Kris Akabussi was trained as a hurdler. For the sake of this analogy, he was brought up like a quarter horse. But when he was brought on to the 4x400 quartet, he adapted. He didn't just make do as a 4x400 runner, he excelled. He trained himself to run like a thoroughbred.

Like Akabussi, you may have been trained for certain conditions, but a time may come when you must shift gears. To succeed at what you're called upon to do, you must be malleable. This doesn't mean you change who you are, it simply means that you must adjust to what the world throws at you. In other words, you must be prepared for the unexpected. In my life, I've found that successful people are the ones who can make adjustments to their plans or behaviors. This key characteristic, another star apple on the tree, is flexibility.

It is my belief that the world has become increasingly difficult to navigate. Looking at my three children, they've had to adjust to a lot more changes than I did when I was kid. I attribute much of this to rapid development and improvement in technology. But no matter how much I want to intercede at times, I try to stand back and let them figure things out for themselves. To adapt and become well-rounded individuals, they need the space to figure out what makes them tick, what speed they want to move at, and how hard they can push themselves. I'm always there to help my kids along the way, but introspection is something they need to learn to do for themselves.

In the corporate setting, I've found that I sometimes need to take a step back and self-assess. We all have mechanisms that come instinctively to us. Once we know what we're good at, we try to use that same skill in every circumstance. But sometimes, those practices just don't fit the given situation and we need to adjust. Many times, I've had to make changes that pushed me outside my comfort zone. I had no choice but to press on and get the work done. Change is difficult, but every time I have adapted to a situation, I've come out on the other end stronger than before.

A good example was when we were working on the Gates Millennium Scholars program while at UNCF. Mr. Gray tapped me to work on pulling together the initial budgets for this landmark $1 billion scholarship program that would benefit approximately 20,000 minority students. The kicker was, we had to get the initial budget together within two weeks, and oh by the way we had to work with three other minority groups to get it accomplished, one of which did not have a formal organization. I remember our first reaction was, "yea right, the world's richest man is going to give us a billion dollars for a scholarship program." The second thought was, how realistic was it for us to get this task accomplished within two weeks.

We trusted Mr. Gray's instincts because we had witnessed him do some amazing things, and make tremendous sacrifices to serve the organization, the member schools, and more importantly: the students. He believed we would get it done. The team pulled all-nighters like we had done back in college, only going home to shower and change clothes. Fast forward to today, the program was launched, and students who were a part of the program are now contributing members of our society. Mr. Gates and his wife Melinda had a vision that was bigger than what most could imagine, but at UNCF we had to adapt to the expectations quick, fast, and in a hurry. We were thoroughbreds during those few weeks, though previously we may have been quarter horses.

I've noticed that the younger generations are far better at this than folks my age and older. Because the world moves so fast, they've learned to adapt along the way. Many young professionals are working jobs that didn't even exist when they were freshmen in college trying to decide on a major. To make it in today's professional world, they've learned to expect the unexpected. If you ask me, I think this has made the younger generations more creative and passionate than any before. For proof, just go on any social media site and see the brands that millennials have created from the ground up. They've had to break norms, rely on their passions, and throw themselves 100 percent into their work. I just wish more people from my generation would embrace their creativity and forward thinking instead of trying to squeeze them into a mold that no longer exists. This generation is thinking like there is no box, and many of us are having to play catch up in many ways. Our experience and wisdom should become guides, not obstacles.

In the corporate setting we have several opportunities to "gut check" on where we stand. There are some things that come instinctively to us, and we try to use them in all situations and circumstances, but oftentimes they don't fit the circumstance, and we are forced to adjust. Those adjustments cause us to step outside of what makes us comfortable, but we must keep pressing on. Who are we in those moments? The thoroughbred or the quarter horse? Just a question.

Therefore, if life becomes scripted by persons who might not know us from a can of paint, what does that mean for us personally. Is that unexpected? Does that truly reflect our character on display at work, home, church, and other social settings? Who are we really? That is the question. I am amazed at how the younger generation seems to process this reality. They are full out 100 percent every time regarding the things that interest them. They pursue their interests to the fullest, even going so far as finding ways to make a living from their inspired passions. They break norms that most managers in the workplace cannot relate to. Unfortunately, rather than leaders shifting to meet this generational trend, the proverbial placing of a square peg into a round hole generally remains the chosen approach. Successful leaders today are the ones who can merge the youth and the seasoned while executing and still driving operational results.

If life were totally scripted, we would never experience the joy of conquering something we thought impossible. And if we could predict the future, some of us would just wait for it to materialize. Others may simply throw up their hands and declare that all outcomes are simply a product of the hand we were dealt. Neither tactic is good. Most of the more enduring moments in our lives, come by way of unexpected lessons that remain etched in our minds forever. Those moments are hard to replace. Being open to learning from life's twists and turns is paramount to seizing the day.

Adventurous people who attempt things others may deem unwise learn to ignore naysayers. Though an adventurer may climb a mountain to experience all life has to offer, others will merely dwell on the fact that they could had died or suffered hypothermia. You see, it's all about perspective, and more importantly being flexible and adapting to change. Putting people into boxes (there goes that box again) and projecting onto them our insecurities and failures is all too prevalent. We end up in conversations where there will never be a meeting of the minds because we are coming to the topic through different lenses. In those moments, many progressive thinkers simply move on and recognize they don't fit the mold. They won't allow themselves to be pigeon-holed into roles dictated by others.

We all have options, but we also must be willing to accept the consequences. If I am a thoroughbred, I can run without a scripted existence and be alright. I am going to run regardless of what folks tell me. If I am a quarter horse, I will eventually experience bursts of speed that will take me the distance in achieving what I want. No limits and no boundaries as I apply that burst of speed. But if I am a donkey, I might simply choose to remain where I am because I am content with having enough grass to eat and water to drink. A scripted life is just fine for some but living up to the standards I set for myself has proven to be far better for me. Take your pick.

From a religious perspective, God laughs while we make plans. We put our plans in pencil, while he writes His in ink. A life sold out for God is never scripted, because we are called to live by faith and not by sight. It is the same concept to some extent.

Whenever I am around my fellow Christian brothers and sisters, we have conversations surrounding our faith. We proudly recite Hebrews 11:1 that reads: "NOW faith is the substance of things hoped for, the evidence of things not seen." But the debate sometimes gets heated when we attempt to discuss faith in the context of contemporary society where faith seems to be attached to logic. We feel a need to see tangible proof. Is that truly faith? I don't think so. Dr. Rudolph McKissick preached a sermon on this same passage of scripture. He shared that when he opened the bible and proceeded to read, the word that jumped out at him was the word, "NOW". In fact, he said he did not even get a chance to move on to the rest of the verse. Somehow, everyone in the congregation that day erupted in praise concerning that single word.

It was amazing to see how people could be moved by the word NOW. I could clearly see the intersection of faith and preparation. Many of those seated in the congregation had been to work all week. They may have had to endure terrible bosses, children acting crazy, a spouse who had lost his or her mind, and even family pets may have presented a challenge. But that day in church, they simply wanted to hear a word suggesting that things would get better. They might not have completely understood how it was going to get better, but they knew that the foolishness they'd endured all week was fleeting and they also knew it would pass.

Where am I going with this? In that historic relay race run by Olympic medal winner Kris Akabussi, he had clearly prepared by training for months on end. He must have restricted his diet, gave up partying, and tried to mentally get himself into a space where he saw himself winning that race. In other words, all the preparation he did gave him faith that he was capable of winning. It is akin to something golf coaches or caddies say as you stand over a shot: "Trust the swing." Though the golfer has undoubtedly practiced by hitting several buckets of balls, he simply needed a reminder that he had prepared for this moment and needed to trust the preparation.

If we could predict our future, we would simply wait for it to unfold. We would be more relaxed and would not spend so much time worried about others, their opinions, or their attempts at *badmind*. What a wonderful existence that would be. But no, we live in a real world peppered with layoffs, illness, disease, egos, and other people's agendas. Thankfully joyous and happy moments, milestones, and accomplishments are also a part of that world. It is all within the soup of life. The intersection of faith and preparedness determine how that soup will taste.

I believe that to feel fulfilled in your work and to reach your greatest potential, you must take risks. This means testing new methods and striving for goals other people believe impossible to achieve. Unfortunately, there will be times when others try to hold you back. For example, you may have a boss who pigeon holes you into a specific role. You'll have to show that person what else you can do and how hard you're willing to work. People aren't simply thoroughbreds or quarter horses. People can train and change based on what they set as their goals and in which race they choose to run. People can be flexible if they want to be.

At times I think back to that day at track practice when I had my outburst. I know now that Coach Moultrie was testing me, but in the moment, it was my own mindset that was keeping me from succeeding. I didn't see myself as a sprinter who needed to use the blocks in the way we were practicing. It felt hopeless. I thought I was a square peg and using the blocks was a round hole. Without faith in my ability to learn the skill, I couldn't get it right during that practice. Essentially, I was undermining myself with my attitude toward the blocks. I was inflexible because I had already made up my mind that this block starting thing was not for me nor was it necessary for my event.

Since then, I've learned to shift my mindset. I have faith that if I prepare properly, I can achieve whatever I set out to do. I've become a planner. Ask my wife, she'll tell you that sometimes I take preparedness to the extreme. After all, I am an accountant. But I've also come to realize that in life, there are things you can't plan for. For those circumstances, I have my faith, and if that is intact, I can be flexible knowing that my efforts will not be in vain.

Faith and preparation complement each other. Through the scriptures, we also learn that "Faith without works is dead." Theologians have discussed and debated this verse to no end, but I choose to take it at face value. I believe that faith and action always go hand in hand.

How many people do you know who are prepared to do great things, but because they lack faith, never try? When I know I am prepared, I choose to act. I know my strengths and what I can achieve, but I also know my limitations and when I'll need help or guidance. Sometimes, I'm the thoroughbred who goes for distance. Other times, I'm the quarter horse who sprints. But I refuse to be the donkey who never races at all.

Chapter Nine

"Son, You Have Three Strikes Against You"

It was early afternoon and our class had just received the results of an accounting exam. I was pleased with my results, but of course with me being hard on myself, I thought I could have done better. After class ended, a couple of us were milling around comparing how we'd done on the test. I rarely like doing this because I believe such comparisons generally lead to students feeling less than adequate. In some of my other classes, that would have been me. Mind you, there were times where we all had a collective "cry in the beer" because all our results were terrible. On this occasion however I opted to join in the conversation. As it turned out several of us from the "islands" had done well, though others had not. I learned that my score was one of the higher ones, and I nervously laughed along with everyone else. It was all in good fun.

Out of the blue, one of my classmates said jokingly: "See, that's why sometimes we don't like having classes with you island folks, because you always mess up the curve." Everyone laughed but to me it felt like nothing more than a backhanded compliment. I laughed nervously nonetheless as I knew it was said in jest. However, I could not let the statement go and it played on my mind. I knew it was supposed to be funny, but I believe that deep down, there was some deep-rooted feeling there and that my classmate must've had a similar experience in other classes for her to say such a thing.

It bothered me to no end. To this day, I don't know why it got under my skin the way it did. I can usually shake things like this off in an instant. Instead of challenging the statement in the moment, I nervously laughed along. Of course, by now you know I was going to have a conversation with Coach Moultrie about it. I was not snitching, but I always respected his opinions as I went through the Mecca. I knew he would put my classmate's comment in perspective for me.

Even before heading over to speak with Coach about the exchange, I reflected on some of the other Caribbean people I'd met on Howard's campus. Some of them were from wealthy homes in their respective countries. Some came to Howard with a suitcase and a dream, and there were many in between. One thing was for certain, the goal was always to get out of there within four years. Many of my African American friends had the same goal. If you got into Howard, it was time to get to work. It was time to "go to the elbows" to finish up strong.

As I was walking over to Coach Moultrie's office, I realized that I'd just had a "dormitory lawyer" experience. Because of my recent arrival, I took it personally because the compliment felt like a put down. I realized nonetheless, that I was caught up in my emotions, as we sometimes get when we feel slighted. "Dormitory lawyers" will cause us to miss the mark every time in terms of what is important.

I visited with Coach and shared the story with him. Instead of sympathy for what I experienced, he gave one of his hearty laughs, then leaned forward in his

112

leather chair. The laughing stopped on a dime however, and he gave me one of those piercing stares. You know, the kind of stare when you know someone has something profound to say, and they must get it out. Peering into my soul again he said, "Son, you have three strikes against you. First you are black. Second, you are young. Third, you are a foreigner. Now what are you going to do with that reality? Do you see these facts as obstacles, or do you see them as stepping stones?"

He then leaned back in his chair and asked me to ponder his question. The room fell silent because I was not sure how to answer as I was trying to tie my indignation following a classmate's relatively mundane comment to this profound question from Coach. For me it was difficult to respond in that moment.

It was time to head out to practice, and I never actually gave him a response to his question. I typically replay his question in my mind whenever I encounter challenges today. It resonated so much with me that at his wake, on the day before his funeral, when I spoke on what Coach meant to me, I brought up this story. There is a video of it floating around on YouTube somewhere that I replay from time to time. Although I never gave him an answer to that question, deep down inside I knew that he was not asking me the question to get an answer. He asked it to shift my perspective. He wanted me to lift my eyes off what was said and see the bigger picture instead. It was not about me, but rather about the person who'd uttered the words. It is not worth it to let folks rent space in our head because for every level we rise to, the harder the challenges will become. Sometimes the challenges are thinly veiled, and might be more hazardous to my family, my career, my finances, my relationships, and so much more. In other words, he was indirectly asking: "So What?"

It was not until later in life that I realized the star apple fruit Coach dropped on me that day was discernment. Discernment to stand in the face of all that is around me and to respond appropriately. Sometimes it is best to not simply agree with nervous laughter, but rather to challenge things that are said that are not true. I've learned to recognize the environment in which I find myself and have learned to figure out methodologies to solve issues, knowing that people who don't know me from a can of paint might have preconceived notions and judgments about me without ever having had a conversation with me.

The three strikes metaphor has been adjusted somewhat now because the strike of being young is gone forever with age. The foreigner aspect is not as prevalent anymore because after being in the United States for almost thirty years, that has diminished. I still get teased that my "twanging" ebbs and flows, but that's okay. The only strike that remains is the fact that I am black. I have been black all my life, and nothing will change that. Is it still a strike? Like I stated before, it depends on one's perspective. That answer lies external to me.

I am a confident person (or so I feel on most days). I carry myself in a dignified manner in any setting. I do not feel inferior to anyone. As far as I am concerned, I put on my pants the same way any other man does. Connections, and cliques might factor in, but for me, I don't see my skin color as a strike. On the other hand, people who have already formed an opinion about me will believe what they want to believe. If verbalized, then *mi ago defend it.* You will not treat me or any member of my family in such a manner. Small minded people are all around, and there are many who are showing their true colors today. It will continue to take discernment to see them for who they truly are given circumstances and situations.

When we were in college, one of my teammates, Shaun Bell, from Tennessee tried to school me on the difference between certain regions of the country. He once asked me if I'd ever been to the South. I said yes, I had been to Fort Lauderdale and Miami. He laughed and asked if I had been to the "Real South." I was puzzled. Today I can also relate the question of the "Real North" because of incidents my family and I experienced while living there. People are people, and they are going to do and say whatever they want to say and do. Once again, the "strike" is in the eye of the beholder.

For five or six years, I worked as the Corporate Controller for the United Negro College Fund, Inc. In this role, I was responsible for the back-office operations for the *An Evening of Stars* telethon. We were stationed in a call center in southern Florida. Over the course of two days I monitored about 300 to 350 agents who took approximately 11,000 phone calls. It was for a worthy cause, and I loved what I did. However, in this space, I also had to step up and handle some very sticky situations that required both courage and discernment, despite wanting to "string some pieces of cloth together." Every year the telethon broadcast was held in the "Real South" on Sunday afternoons. In some cases, it took place right after the church hour and in others it was right around dinner time.

Like clockwork each year I would huddle with the managers at the call center, and speak with the agents taking the calls. I told them that they would hear some stuff on the calls that they should just ignore. Some of the agents had "virgin ears" in regards to how they would be challenged by what some of the callers might say.

Only a small fraction of the calls were offensive, but invariably we would get that call where the opening question would be, "why are you n#@&%$ on my television?" or the classic, "what would happen if WE set up a United White College Fund?" There were other variations of those questions and comments. We would just smile as if they were standing right in front of us, and try to diffuse the situation. As for the more troubling calls---I would take those. I stayed in the control room so I could listen in on some of the conversations for training purposes. I must admit that sometimes it made me upset that in that day and time (circa 1998 through 2004) people still felt the way they did. That was a bit of naivete on my part back then as I soon learned that much of the entire nation harbored some ill-will towards people of color. The crazy thing is that sometimes they had no idea why they felt that way.

When Dr. Dorothy Cowser Yancy offered me an opportunity to come down to Johnson C. Smith University to be her Chief Financial Officer, my first instinct was to turn her down because it meant I'd have to move to North Carolina, which is the "Real South." Ignorance abounded based on what I had been told, and seen on television. Then, when I lived in Upstate New York, in what was supposed to be a totally progressive part of the country, I also encountered some of the "Real South." Fast forward to our current climate regarding race relations in this country. Today we see the hand-wringing and questioning in terms of how we could still be here? We also hear carefully worded statements proclaiming that we live in a post racial society. It is not until I lived in upstate New York that I truly appreciated this quote attributed to Malcolm X: "The southern United States is anywhere south of the Canadian border."

In today's dispensation in time, we are going to have to develop the discernment to tackle this issue. Life is not a class that is graded. There is no curve to be messed up, but the way people relate to each other will be shaped by how we deal with this matter of race once and for all. As with the calls we received during the telethon, people who make racist comments are in the minority, but because of the outrageous nature of what they say and believe those calls were the ones we remembered the most. The same is true with society at large. We allow small groups who peddle such beliefs to have the largest voice.

We need courage and discernment to engage in tough conversations. We need to live in someone else's shoes for a moment or two. To Coach's point, we can use this issue of race relations as a stumbling block or a steppingstone to properly heal as a nation and global community. The question out there for all of us to answer is: "Who is going to lead us through these difficult conversations?" The answer is obvious. It is the person we see staring back at us in the mirror each morning.

While the telethons took place some time ago, not much has improved. We continue to live in a system fraught with institutional racism and we still live side by side with people who are overtly prejudiced, yet smile at us. Some will argue that everyone, regardless of the color of their skin, has equal legal rights in the United States, so how could we not be equal? The people who believe this benefit most from the lie. If they tell themselves it's true, then they don't have to act on the inequality; they don't have to do the work and fight for true social equality. By pointing to legal rights and ignoring reality, people don't have to deal with the underlying ugliness of persistent racism that some of us still experience. People create their own reality so they don't have to face actuality. It is not uncommon for someone who never experiences racism to believe that it no longer exists. After all, they've never been on the receiving end of bigotry. Race-relations around the globe won't improve without a reckoning. We can't fix what we won't face.

Many of our nation's leaders benefit from this deception. They don't honestly acknowledge the hardships and mistreatment their constituents face. Many of them haven't experienced our country's deepest problems like poverty and racial discrimination and don't see the urgency of tackling these issues. Take for example the recent admissions scandal in higher education. For years individuals decried the efforts of institutions that tried to balance the admission standards by admitting people of color to colleges and universities. We learned of lawsuits filed by aggrieved parties who saw this as inappropriate as it might deny access to those who *rightly* belong in said institutions. Legacy admissions and other practices were ignored in the lawsuits. What the recent admissions scandal, and all its derivatives to date, highlighted was the double standard whereby the rich and influential get their way, while others have to play by the rules.

Also, notable, is the punishment being proposed for those involved in the recent admissions scandal. Compare and contrast a young woman from Akron, Ohio who is spending five years in prison for sending her children to the wrong school district in order to eke out a better education for them. While in the current admissions scandal, in one case the sentence handed down to a celebrity, who paid an administrator of the SAT, to cheat on her daughter's test, was a mere 14 days.

During a recent heart-to-heart conversation with a Caucasian colleague we concluded that the reason some of our white brothers and sisters don't speak up when it comes to inequalities, is due to a palpable fear we've sensed for years: They fear that if people of color get into power and have an opportunity to dictate the way things are done, there will be some sort of payback for what was done to our ancestors throughout history.

Especially as it relates to the injustices of the Transatlantic Slave Trade and Jim Crow laws. Although a heartfelt comment by my colleague, it confirmed what many people of color believe is the case: Some of our Caucasian brothers and sisters believe the boogeyman is around the corner, and if he gets too close to making changes, their way of life will be threatened forever. That might be the most striking reason this topic is always placed on the back burner, and not fully addressed. If we were in a society that openly discusses these issues, the fearful would see that this is the furthest thing from folks' minds. We simply all want to live and enjoy this thing called life. The systems that have been set up are hiding in plain sight, and they are still having the same corrosive effects they did back in the 1940s, 1950s, and 1960s.

Although there is a sense that racism will dissipate over time, it's not the case. As I mentioned before, we really cannot fix what we won't face, and we are running out of time for engaging in constructive conversations that address the issues. I could probably list several systems and practices that created this imbalance, but being solution oriented, I strongly believe that the issues first need to be placed on the table for discussion. This requires strong and compassionate leaders, who are not beholden to any one group to get this done right.

In the past, much that comes up for discussion or a point around which we can all coalesce has been shot down. Partly because of a lack of understanding and acknowledgement of how the systems are designed to work against people of color. As I've said before, it is difficult, when that change is tied to power.

Additionally, it is very difficult to think big when small has you in its grasp. For example, the *Black Lives Matter* movement was started to address police brutality. That was quickly coopted with *All Lives Matter*. We speak of gentrification and the destruction of communities, only to be asked to move our institutions, like my alma mater Howard University, so that neighbors can do as they please. We talk about the historical inequality of funding and access to institutions of higher education only to be told that quotas and select funding should be abolished without noting that HBCUs and other Minority Serving Institutions were created due to exclusionary practices in the past. These institutions must go to court to get past issues remedied.

Don't get me wrong, a lot of great leaders have used their privilege and their voice to lift up others, but the most revolutionary social movements grew from the ground up, starting with people who faced hardship themselves. Look at Martin Luther King Jr., Marcus Garvey, Rosa Parks, Medgar Evers, Nelson Mandela, and Thurgood Marshall, for example. Given what we are currently witnessing globally the tenets and concepts espoused by Marcus Garvey seem more attractive now than ever. To some, it is clear that people of color will only rise from this perceived quagmire of mediocrity and averageness if we take a renewed sense of pride in what we own and move it to the next level. Our black pride does not dictate that we should exclude ourselves for the collective society, but rather we must recognize that we have to keep the core strong in order to drive the improvements we must make. That core is strengthened when we know who we truly are when faced with efforts meant to: "Put people of color in their place." Knowing who we are strengthens us in such a way that we become comfortable in any space, with any person, at any time. Our courage will keep us there when others want to flee.

As constituents, it behooves us to harness the collective power of the court of public opinion. Regardless of our political party affiliations, religious beliefs, or socioeconomic status, we all want leaders we can trust. Together, we need to keep the people in power, regardless of sphere, accountable for their actions and call out wrongdoings regardless of what side of the aisle or group they come from.

In turn, it is important that we work harder at understanding each other. Platforms such as Twitter and Facebook provide us with a common stage upon which to communicate and share ideas. Through social media, we get to hear a diverse mix of opinions and perspectives. Online, people can share their needs and what changes they want to see. It should humble us and make us more compassionate towards one another, but it doesn't seem to. Instead, we use online platforms to argue and antagonize one another. Rather than seeking out alternative points of view, we follow people online who share and amplify the opinions we already hold. We draw lines in the sand and then lies and misinformation deepen the divide between us. Instead, we need to engage in open, honest conversations regarding the current climate.

If we are discerning about our approach not only to this issue, but all issues that have merit in driving change in our world, we can make the turn for the better. Discernment is needed to truly identify those who just need the extra push to get into the ring, but we are truly in this thing together (pick any topic). When we fail to see the beauty of the human spirit in each of us, those who want to have us at constant logger heads will continue to win. During my time in upstate New York I met some great people of all races. Many of them are my friends to this day. We exchange ideas all the time surrounding how we might make this world better. What Coach Moultrie said was so true. What we see as stumbling blocks are stepping stones, but we have to want to step together, especially when some of those stones are not firmly planted. Discernment, coupled with courage make up the difference. Are you willing to take that step? Don't answer now, just ponder the question.

HOWARD UNIVERSTY TRACK AND FIELD

Coach Named Full-time

John Mitchell
Hilltop Staff Reporter

Howard University Track and Field Coach William Moultrie has a challenge posted on the door to his office that reads:

"You must run here or...run away from here."

On August 1, of this year, Coach Moultrie was appointed as Howard's full-time coach, after coaching 12 years under part-time status. He considers his appointment as a very exciting one.

"I'm excited because the appointment gives me better latitude and an opportunity to better service track athletes academically and athletically," said Moultrie. He added, "I'm looking forward to the athletes doing a better job."

Coach Moultrie, a native of Rockdale, Texas and a graduate of Texas Southern University, has compiled an impressive record since coming to Howard in 1973. He has coached 47 All-Americas, all of whom have graduated. Last year, eight Bison tracksters qualified for the Olympic trials. Three of them, Ruperta Charles, Anton Skerritt and Richard Louis took part in the games.

Moultrie also helped long jumpers Theresa Allen and Brenda Bailey achieve All-America status earlier this year.

However, Coach Moultrie made it perfectly clear that the highlight of his career came with his appointment to the U.S. Olympic Track and Field Staff in 1984. Just recently, he was chosen as national co-chairman for sprints and relays in the United States.

With all of these accomplishments behind him, one would think that the coach should be satisfied. He isn't.

"I'm not satisfied because when you become satisfied that's when it becomes time to get out of coaching," said Moultrie.

When asked what's left for him to do at Howard, Moultrie said, "Three to five years from now I would like to see the team win the NCAA Track and Field Championship, or at least be a strong contender for the title. As full-time coach, I will be able to recruit the caliber of kids that can make this possible."

Track head coach William Moultrie looking for improvement.

Track Coach, Howard University

125

Howard Bisons

Gerald Hector

William P. Moultrie

Annual Awards Ceremony

Graduation Day

Coach

Coach Imparting Wisdom

Bison Reunion

Coach, Mentor, Father Figure, Friend

Chapter Ten

Son, when it's Breezy, Swing it Easy

The year is 1997, two of my friends, Donald Christian and Oliver McIntosh were heading out to play golf. Oliver was down from Harvard to spend a weekend in Washington DC. I had never played golf before, so I was about to head home and tell them that I would catch up with them later. I had no interest in playing golf, because if you take the clubs away, I would just be out for a walk. Plus, the fact that I played *real* sports. I played football (what most call soccer), cricket, and ran track. Golf to me was not a sport. It was for middle aged, overweight men, and others who were either fully or semi-retired. Once again, ignorance is bliss. Now that I am bit wiser, I do realize "that a cup of wisdom a day prevents idiot decay." I often wonder who I should attribute that quote to. Nevertheless, I grabbed my keys and headed towards my car. Oliver is always the "vibes" man. He said, "*No man a wah you a do.* Come play some golf man." Still not interested, I found every excuse in the book. Back home in Jamaica we called them "*bowling bouncers.*" None that was bowled had its desired effect. In the end, I had to push past my preconceived notions about the game. I fought with every fiber, but the guilt trip overcame me and I gave in. "If anything, you going to hang out with your *bredrens.*" With my arm severely twisted behind my back, I went.

We drove into the parking lot of the Enterprise Golf Course in PG County, Maryland. The drive from the main road was exactly what I expected. Farmland entrance, with a Great House for entertaining and

131

nestled in a corner was the clubhouse. I owned no golf clubs, and all I came armed with was a *"yam licking"* swing from my days of being a lower order batsman on my cricket team. I had good hand eye coordination, so I thought I would be fine. I would hold my own I thought. After all, I have never seen a challenge I could not overcome. If someone else had accomplished it before, I could do it as well. Up to that point I did not know the different loft on each club. I just thought it was fine to get one club, and make my way around. If I wanted to hit the ball far, I'd swing harder. If I had a shorter shot, swing softer. How difficult was that. If I had enough strikes of the ball, I would eventually get to each green. Simple. Or so I thought.

I rented a set of clubs (or maybe I played with either Don's or Oliver's). I had no golf shoes. I had on some Nike sneakers. I felt like a real *"neva si come si."* I had no golf etiquette. I just had manners from my upbringing. I had to follow instructions from my two friends to not embarrass myself on the course. My biggest fear was that there would be people gathered around the first tee box, or any tee box for that matter. My pride could not take a beating. To this day I am thankful there were no camera phones available. I would definitely be on YouTube with multiple hits. The only thing I did well that day was to pose nicely after each shot. Or what looked like a shot.

Needless to say, I played soldier golf (left and right) for the entire round. I don't remember the score. Let's just say I was there to hang out with my friends. The score was not important. That is all that needs to be said on that topic. It was absolutely terrible. The hand eye coordination does not help when you have to regulate your hips, keep your spine at the right angle and rotate around it, and also make sure that my hips did not get ahead of my hands, all the while making sure that my head stayed behind the ball. With all of those instructions, I opted to simply play one or two cover drives. I played at least two pull shots through mid-wicket, and I kid you not, at one point it felt as if I played a square drive off the back foot. That is all I knew. That is what Roy McClean taught us at the nursery down at my high school, Kingston College, in Jamaica. Now you probably have some sense of what that final score looked like...

As miserable as it seemed, there was the one and only one bright spark. I hit one shot with the driver on the back nine. That one shot was perfect. So pure that I did not feel the ball leave the clubhead. I followed all the instructions to a "T", but I thought it was pure luck. Oliver told me to transfer my weight to my right leg, and when I was taking the club back down, follow through while shifting my weight forward. Well, that seemed to me to be the same concept of a front foot drive in cricket. The only difference was that I had to remember my head and spine. Somehow it came together. When I hit the ball, the recorded version of the comments cannot be written here, but it ended with "...*claaat*." I was told to keep my head down, and they would look where the ball went. Now that expression was not from me, so I imagined it was a good shot. I felt nothing. The shot was so pure, that I thought I'd missed the ball completely. You see when you are a "*yam licker*" from the lower level of the batting order in cricket, you tend to swing at almost everything, and that is usually done with your eyes closed.

I received further confirmation that it was a good shot when I heard, "*yow dat wicked. Straight down the middle.*" I thought that was a lie because to that point, after hitting my tee shot, I had to make my way over to either the water, or the woods. One thing was certain, they enjoyed my company because of the number of balls I retrieved from the woods while looking for mine. All three shots were played, and we hopped in the carts to play our second shots. We came up on the first ball, but it wasn't mine. We came up on the second ball, and it wasn't mine. I could not see any more balls on the fairway, so I retrieved my seven iron to go start another round of searching in the woods. Both Don and Oliver shouted, "*a weh yuh a guh?*" I replied "to look for my ball." They said, "no man, your ball must be further up." Further up? At that point I started saying to myself, "*dem tek man fi eediat.*" I decided to play along. About another twenty yards up, and just off to the edge of the fairway I saw a little white dot. I thought to myself, "that must be a piece of paper." As I got closer, the paper looked rounder and rounder, and the confirmation came with a shout, "*si your ball ova de suh.*"

I had to catch myself, because this ball was way down the fairway. It was a about 110 yards left of the pin. Now in my more mature years of playing golf, that is a regular thing to hit driver and pitching wedges into shorter par four holes. However, my perspective as a "*yam licker*" playing for the first time, I was overjoyed. My elation was punctuated by the fact that I hit the ball so cleanly that I did not feel it vibrate through the club.

It was a pure swing. To this day I am trying to recreate that feeling. After hundreds of golf rounds that all cost money, equipment, clothing, lessons, and prayers, I have not been able to replicate neither that feeling nor that swing. Today, I play golf simply for enjoyment. On that day however, the sensation I felt by hitting a shot like that is all I remember. I quickly forgot my many excursions into the bushes and sand traps. All that stuck with me is that I needed to come back again and recapture that feeling.

The golf bug had bitten me hard. I went home and told Sharon. I guess the sheer joy she saw on my face, prompted her to go get me my first set of Wilson starter clubs. I was so grateful for the clubs, though I was confused as to why she'd bought them. You see, she bought the clubs two weeks before our first son was born. I was grateful for the gift, but deep down inside I was like, *"why yuh buy dem yah fah. When mi ago get fi play when di youth born?"* My wife responded, "you will find some time every now and then." She's been my baby for twenty-five years of marriage and she understands that sports run in my blood.

As fate would have it, an opportunity to play golf came up when some family and friends came into town to see the baby. Neither of them played golf, and I could not find anyone else. At wits end, I said to myself, I could go and try to play by myself with these starter clubs. However, if they put me in a group with strangers, I ran the risk of being laughed off the course. To that end, I thought of the best strategy. I always heard that Coach Moultrie was a golf fanatic. He would do anything for a game of golf. He had one rule though:

135

He did not play golf on Sundays. That day was reserved solely for worship at church.

We settled on a Saturday afternoon at the Needwood Golf Course in Montgomery County, Maryland. I had it all figured out. If we were a twosome, and we got to the course and they wanted to pair us up with two more players, I could easily keep calling him coach, and the other players would know that I was just learning. That way, if there were any excursions into the woods, sand traps, or water hazards, they would know that I was being coached, and that I had not been playing long. Genius!

We arrived at the golf course separately. When I got there, as usual, Coach was already there waiting. He never ever wanted to be late. I pulled up and took out my newly minted golf bag, stuffed with my Wilson starter clubs. The accessories were on point. Nike golf shoes, shorts, shirt, belt, and hat. The socks were a different brand. I had gone to the driving range a couple of times, but after each trip, I washed and polished the clubs. They were clean. Whenever I pulled a club, you heard "schwing" just like a samurai sword being pulled from its sheath. I was ready to do battle at Needwood Golf Course. Coach just stared at me. I knew he wanted to laugh. He had always said that Howard graduates were a little bit too cocky, but he would hurriedly qualify that by saying we had every right to be that way. You can tell who they are a mile away. He said, "Hector it looks like you are ready Son. Your outfit looks good, but let's see how you hit this ball. One other thing, I don't speak much while I play. Any speaking you hear will be my way of motivating myself. If you ask me questions, I will answer them when we get back to clubhouse."

When he said that, my calm, cool, and collected state of mind disappeared. I was witnessing the competitive side of coach which few had seen while playing a sport with him. I then replayed my last few results at the driving range. The *"yam licking"* was a hallmark. That did not get replaced, though there were less direct hits straight to the left or right. They more like faded or hooked to the left or right with less aggression than before. I felt confident that I could step up on the tee box and go to work. I didn't have much of a short game because I spent the range time on the driver and irons, trying to replicate that first shot at Enterprise. Another bit of good news came my way. We were going to be sent out as a twosome. I also knew that the Lord looks out for fools and babies. I wasn't a baby so that left the other option. We loaded up our golf cart and headed out to the first tee.

My golf shoes were so new, they felt crispy, and every time I took a step they squeaked. I just hoped that would not be a distraction. What was weird was as we started driving to the tee box, Coach got very quiet. I gave him the honor of hitting first because he was Coach, and I had so much respect for him. Truth be told, I wanted to see what I was up against, and how tight I had to keep my game. He stepped up whistling, and started talking to himself, or his ball, or something. He kept saying "okay puppy, let's do this." He had just bought the Taylor Made driver, and he was going to give it a run. His backswing was something I saw some of the young people do at the driving range. Full rotation.

Head steady. Spine straight. His first tee shot was butter. As he retrieved his tee, my entire confidence shifted. It took everything in me to utter "good shot." I knew I had gotten myself into something I could not get out of at this point. I summoned all the golf gods to allow me to make a good showing.

I stepped up to the tee box, shoes squeaking all the way. New shorts with creases similar to the edge of a knife. New hat turned backwards. I placed my tee into the ground, and the yam licking mindset grabbed a hold of me immediately. I felt every muscle in my body engage because I was not about to let Coach outdrive me on the very first hole. I had to set the tone early on. He might be accurate with his irons and his approach shots, but there was no way I was going to let him out drive me. That was the wrong focus from the first tee box, but I knew no better. After my swing, I headed to the woods just off the fairway to commence the customary search for my ball. Coach on the other hand, just started whistling and drove off down the middle of the fairway. Meanwhile, there I was taking commands from the golf sergeant, "Left, Right, Left, Right." It was a depressing scene and we'd only just begun the round.

By the fourth or fifth hole, I realized that when he said he was not going to talk, he meant about the round. On the other hand, we talked about life after Howard. My career in public accounting, and the family. He really took an interest in what I was doing. It was cool to hang out with Coach four years after graduation and I was reminded of all those times I sat in the chair against the wall in his office.

As the round progressed, it became overcast and windy. Hurricane type windy to be exact (or so it seemed to a golfer). With the change in conditions, and a strong breeze blowing across the course, my natural instincts kicked in. I told myself that with each upcoming shot, I would have to power the ball through the wind in order to get more distance. That meant, I had to up the power in my swing on the "yam licking." The muscling up on the first tee, was nothing compared to the muscling up on almost every shot on the back nine because of the wind. After each shot, I went searching in the woods, sand traps, or using a ball retriever from the water. Nothing new. Coach on the other hand was hitting down the middle, chip and putt. I did not hit one green in regulation, but I know for sure that Coach hit almost all of them. Truth be told, that was frustrating to watch and experience. I even thought that the only reason I did not erupt was because of my great respect for the man. I am a fierce competitor, but I am not accustomed to taking butt whoopings like that, especially from someone who went about whistling while making shot after shot look so easy.

I labored on for eighteen holes. Parts of the round are still a blur to me. After the round, just like my first outing at Enterprise, the scorecard was not my focus. I just wanted to get home and get out of my "outfit", eat some humble pie, and regroup for the week ahead. I wanted to get home and play with my newborn son. At least he would not know anything about the butt whooping I had just taken. I also had every intention of asking the Lord in church the next day, what went wrong.

After Coach dropped me off at my vehicle, he said, "are you going to get something to eat Hector?" Not wanting to sound like I was brushing him off, I said, "sure." I can't recall where we ended up going, but it gave us an opportunity to just talk. Oddly enough, the conversation turned to the round of golf and how I had played. He was not my golf coach, but he will always be Coach. He was always the technician, and he constantly reminded us, "if you are going to do something Son, do it right. To do it right you have to practice right. If you practice bad habits, you will get bad results. Quit making stuff hard Son." He explained to me about my set up at address, my posture, my rotation, and head positioning (all the things Oliver and Don had told me). He also launched into a common sense approach at course management while playing.

I was soaking it all in, because I had heard it before from my friends, but this was coach Moultrie. A man who had guided me ever since I set foot in the United States. It was during this after golf conversation that he uttered the words that I continue to apply to life today. He said, "Son, golf is a game of opposites. You believe because you are young and strong that you can simply muscle through the ball by swinging hard. How many times did your drives hit the fairway? Don't answer. I know. Aside from swinging too hard, you did not assess your surroundings. On the back nine the weather changed. The winds started blowing. You made no adjustments. You probably thought to yourself that you could hit the ball through the wind. Well you see how much further your ball was blown off line? Don't answer. I know."

This wasn't the chair alongside the wall in his office, but it might as well have been. He was dropping knowledge, and I was tracking right along with him because I had spent four years under this tutelage. I had figured out all his sayings, then out of nowhere he dropped this little gem: "Son, when it is breezy. You have to swing it easy. Use the winds to help you shape the shot. You cannot fight the wind Son, use it instead." I promise you, to this day I do not remember another word he said after that. The simplicity of it just stopped me in my tracks (or eating in this case). He was correct. I made no adjustments when conditions changed. It was not like I was playing a stellar round and the driving wind had me playing worse on the back nine. The lesson in it for me was though the winds blew, I did not have the presence of mind to adapt to the change. I just kept doing the same things I'd tried to teach myself at the driving range. If the wind was behind me, or helping, I swung just as hard. I then would think, "I hit with the pitching wedge, and the ball traveled as far as with an eight iron." Now I know why, and understand that the opposite is also true when hitting into the wind. I know I must have torn my undergarments swinging as hard as I did on three holes trying to power the ball through the wind, with disappointing results.

Today, with the gift of hindsight, I was as wrong as two left shoes, but I was stuck in my own pride and wanting to do things my way. I thought I had taught myself to play the game, though there might be an off chance that I was too cheap to pay for lessons. After all, I am an athlete, and thought I could figure it out on my own. In short, I guess it was safe to say that I lacked humility. The bible tells us that pride comes before the fall. Although I did not fall, I did not score well. The law of averages says that a young twenty something should be able to beat a person pushing on seventy years of age in an athletic (albeit semi athletic) event.

Returning to our star apple tree, the derivative fruit here is humility. Just because you perceive you have the power to do something, does not necessarily mean you should ignore the basics. We often do what we want because there is no governor on what we say, nor on what we want to accomplish. Left to our own devices we will plow through everything leaving damage in our wake. Sometimes we are just wrong but we keep pushing despite the warning signs. In my case that day, the breeze was blowing everything off line; however, I did not make any adjustments. I just kept pushing through. That overblown sense of self-worth leads to arrogance that if left unchecked can cause all sorts of challenges for us in our relationships and regards to our life goals.

On the Island Alone

I can imagine coach's thoughts all the way from heaven and can almost hear him in a cosmic conversation with me...

Coach: Hector, over the course of my life, I have come to understand that no man is an island, and no man stands alone. I know there are songs that carry this title, and it is a cliché that many utter. However, I don't think too many of us have taken it to heart. They are just words that roll off our tongue, without impact. The focus on the self in western society causes us to think that way.

Now I am not saying that we as individuals don't have a responsibility to address this phenomenon, but I am saying that we have been conditioned in this manner. Community to some is absent, and the old familiar expression, "pull yourself up by your bootstraps" is the main order of the day. I promise you I dislike when people say that. They are forgetting from whence they came. They love to project that they are more accomplished than what people see.

There is an unintended haughtiness that accompanies our thoughts when we remain in this place. I am reminded of individuals who live by the motto, "there is no one alive who can tell me anything." We call them narcissists. We call them all kinds of names that I can't repeat here. However, before we get too high and mighty ourselves, we should acknowledge that there is a little of that in each of us. Being self-centered can drive us forward, however, when it gets to the level where that's all we believe, we have a problem. It is in these moments that we become blinded by our own light. Put more pointedly in the words of grandmas, and mothers of the churches, "you start smelling yourself." Think of it this way. You don't appreciate a good boss, until you have had a bad one. Unfortunately, some of us cut our teeth on a boss who was domineering, conceited, and lacking humility. We have to be careful we do not mistreat the good boss because we have been conditioned by the bad one.

I know I might not be making much sense here because we've been taught to go for broke. Get all you can get for you and your family. Laudable? Yes. However, the means we see employed today are downright scary.

People are waking up to it now, and are demanding different, but don't know how to effect change. Therefore, those in power continue to force their agenda on everyone despite the "winds of change." Take the United States for example. The changing demographics is embraced by most of the population, but there is a remnant who want to remain in the past. I use the word remnant on purpose, because some of the so-called Christians in our society are the ones who would like to keep everyone right where they are. They have become a group of individuals who are now on an island by themselves, but here is the kicker, they have the economic power, and the "complexion for protection."

My sense of all of this comes from a recent article I saw you reading from ChristianPost.com. The article was entitled, "Most White Evangelicals Say Immigration, Increasing Racial Diversity Harms America." If the headline wasn't jarring enough, the article goes on to state the following: "When asked about the growing number of "newcomers" to the United States, white evangelicals (57 percent) were the only major religious group with a majority stating that immigrants "threaten traditional American customs and values." Whose values are they referring to? The Native Americans? The Irish? The African Americans? The Asians? They seem to have forgotten that the United States has always been a nation of immigrants. The winds of change are blowing, but now instead of adjusting and adapting, they are now more inclined to go get the driver for a fifty-yard shot in order to plow through the winds to make a decent score. They are swinging that driver in close quarters with several people standing around. They eventually are going to have challenges in scoring because there are variables they cannot control. Some want to play God.

To that end, as the melting pot of the United States, and I would say the entire world continues to diversify, we should be mindful of those who historically held the power, and now believe it's slipping away. If they could carve out their own enclaves around the globe they would. That still does not change the fact that the winds are blowing. Now, if they would simply adapt and adjust their thinking, and allow for the melting pot to provide for them in a different way, the fear and anxiety they have would not be so daunting. Because they have not taken the time to adapt to the change, or to put it another way, they are not using the changes to assist them in life, they are more comfortable being on their own island, communities and enclaves, and fighting against the wind. They only want results designed to break down established norms of humanity to get their way. It is a sad thing to see, especially when you know they are operating from a standpoint of ignorance, hatred, and fear. If you don't believe me, look at the run up to the midterm elections of 2018. I rest my case...

There are 66 books in the bible, and I have studied most of them. I must say I continue to marvel at the ways in which we continue to use the scriptures to manipulate people. Claiming it says things it clearly does not and driving more people away with messages that are totally contrary to the teachings of Jesus Christ. Instead of being a welcoming force of change, we have used religion and spirituality as another wind generator to drive division. It is not sustainable by any stretch of the imagination. I pray for leaders who are committed to use the winds of change to reframe a discussion about our common humanity. They are the leaders who will spend time in communities and spaces that may be unfriendly towards them. Not to say that they checked something off a list, but to actively listen, be vulnerable, and take action requires authentic sacrifice. I refuse to believe that God created us all but did not create the wisdom necessary to make this world more inviting for everyone. Greed, coupled with a lack of humility, will continue to cause us to falter. We keep hearing about the next great generation, but how can we be great in the future, if our foundation right now is rocky and unbalanced. We simply continue to arrogantly suggest that we know what is right. I fear we are stuck with a driver in our hands trying to hit hundred-yard shots, while trying to adjust the way we use the club, even though it is not designed for that purpose. We have a mismatch of priorities and no matter how we try; we have made this thing so difficult.

There is An Eye in The Storm

Following my cosmic conversation with Coach Moultrie, I have come to some conclusions of my own. In 1988 I lived through Hurricane Gilbert in Jamaica. I recall prior to it hitting the island I had always been fascinated by hurricanes and storms. The elders in my immediate circle would talk about them with such glee. Utterances like, *"wi not even did have wata afterwards, and the whole place mash up."* For some reason I wanted to witness such devastation. Why? Only God knows. It is like being addicted to those YouTube videos where you know the outcome, but watch any way. There is some sick joy in seeing something that scares the mess out of us. After experiencing Gilbert, I had my fill of destructive storms.

I was a teenager when the storm hit, and I, like any hardheaded teenager, went outside while the storm was raging. In my community of Aylsham in Kingston 6, the homes were built close together. They were lined up in pathways and the rows of houses were separated by parks and free flowing areas. Silly me thinking that if I stuck close to the buildings one could still walk around. Yes, it was possible, and we did, but it was incredibly dangerous. The winds were extremely fierce, and you could see large objects blowing all around us. Being a neophyte to all things hurricane related, I was strangely impressed by how strong the winds were while I stood on the leeward side of the houses and watched the destruction. I thought to myself, "how long can this wind be sustained like this?" My memory is not the greatest right now, but I think the first wave lasted a couple of hours. I say first wave because at the midpoint came the eye of the hurricane.

I remember the eye vividly because it was in the middle of a beautiful sunny day. I was puzzled. A couple of hours ago the winds and driving rain had us worried out of our minds as to whether our shingled roofs would hold up. Here we were in the eye of the hurricane, and things were calm. I took the opportunity to step out into the broad daylight and mostly blue skies to tour the neighborhood. I went around to my girlfriend's house to see how things were. While standing on the side lawn of her family's house chatting

147

in the relative warmth and dryness of the eye, I saw her neighbor come outside with a machete. He climbed a coconut tree in his yard and commenced to cut down some young coconuts that were not yet ripened. The horror of seeing the *"jelly dem"* being cut down before they had matured was troubling (as I might have requested a couple in the future), but I would soon discover there was a method to his madness. He was doing a good thing. He was removing young coconuts from the tree because given the strength of the winds we'd just experienced, they could become projectiles. In other words, the first round of winds presented a challenge. During the subsequent calm, he adjusted and prepared for the second round of winds. At a minimum, these young coconuts would not be able to cause additional damage.

In my young years, I did not see these events in that light. Now a bit older, I had to look no further than living in Ithaca, New York for this metaphor to manifest for me again. As I mentioned before in a previous chapter, it was the fall of 2015, and racial tensions were exploding on college campuses all across America. The genesis some will argue was at the University of Missouri. It spread like wildfire. Presidents were asked to step down. Higher education leaders found themselves trying to answer questions on a topic they had given marginal attention to. At a minimum, those who had the power to make changes did not have a lived experience, and the list goes on and on. It is in that context that I had a discussion with a faculty member at Ithaca College. This professor had lived in the area for a good part of his life. He was a member of the local school board and was an advocate for racial healing and understanding in the city.

He came and spoke to my staff and I on this topic. He shared a detailed history of race relations in the town, and the nucleus of why we were where we were. It was a powerful presentation. The "oohs and aahs" from the attendees suggested that people were getting it. For some it was shocking. For others it was confirmation. For some it was the opening of old wounds. I was fully engaged, learning everything I could. I juxtaposed what I heard to my lived experiences in Jamaica, Trinidad and Tobago and the United States. My pastor, Nathaniel Wright, in each sermon he preached there was always a problem part of the text. And true to form, though it was a rich dialogue, along came the part of the discussion that was a problem for me. It stemmed from this statement: "It seems like every ten years we have a racial issue at the high school. It is like clockwork." I saw people reflecting and the usual nodding of heads in agreement. I also heard the slight clapping of hands acknowledging that some great truth had just been shared.

The discussion moved on but I was stuck. I couldn't help but think; "so if this happens every 10 years or so like clockwork, what have we done to shift the narrative?" Simply moving past the statement and the lack of reaction from others bothered me. It suggested that over the years, we had not become the change we wanted to see in this small town. The winds of adversity had blown before, but instead of using the winds of change to our advantage, could it be that there were some who basically fought against the winds and

149

won? I had too many questions. Now that the winds had arisen again, what were we going to do this time? Were we going to be courageous enough to do like my girlfriend's neighbor during Hurricane Gilbert and cut down some of the coconuts hanging on the tree during the eye of the storm, before the second round of winds came? I was actively on the lookout for that to happen. It did not. What were some of the "coconuts" we could have cut down? I would say indifference, unfamiliarity with the culture of others, intolerance of differing views, the embracing of others who might have come from a different part of the country for starters. Intolerance was easily veiled because one of the world's greatest universities is in the town, and it is also home to another prestigious college. While sitting in such a bubble, it is hard to pause for a moment to realize that the very things we criticize others of doing outside our confines is actually taking place inside our bubble.

Well, just like clockwork (I am not sure if it was the ten-year mark exactly), another racial incident flared up at the high school. This time it was over acting parts in a play. Two of my children signed a petition concerning the incident. My wife and I observed from a distance as our children engaged for the first time in a meaningful way on this topic. We were so proud because we never hid this sordid issue from them, and our being pleased solely had to do with the fact that they are going to be living in this world, where being passed over for roles in a play is a microcosm of what they will potentially face. This town presented for us all an incubator where we could work in the eye of the storm to see how we could chart a way forward. Could we be a model for the nation? In my utopian view, yes, we could. Did we? I am not so sure. We had more meetings, more programs, and more discussions. However, what is needed is the cutting down of coconuts that could potentially cause damage in the future.

Unfortunately, the issue was not fully resolved and we simply started the clock on another 10-year cycle. With the elections of 2016 and since, the coconuts are now mature, and they are huge. They have become much larger projectiles capable of causing much more damage. Well true to form, we will wait for another incident to occur, then we will cut one coconut down, get at its contents to soothe us, and everything will be back to normal.

If the eye of the hurricane taught me anything, it is that we should get to work when we experience the damaging effects of the first wave of winds. In the eye, we need to make assessments of the damage that occurred, and determine how we might repair that damage, but more importantly remove anything else that could become a threat when the second wave of wind arrives. Here is our problem in society today: we do none of that. The gains made in the civil rights era are steadily being usurped. Just think about this: we are still talking about the Voting Rights Act in 2018. We witnessed blatant attempts in the mid-term elections of 2018 to suppress the votes of people of color. The same folks who stood by in the 50's, 60's, and 70's, are still hoping the winds of change will blow over. Nothing is new under the sun. It just comes back in a different package. Unfortunately for many of us, we have opened the package and don't like what we see. However, we can't return it and have become stuck on a treadmill of sorts.

I remain hopefully optimistic that my children's generation will prick the conscience of this nation and the world. However, the number of people of color, biracial young people, and a host of other variables that were not present in the past, force us all to stop and take a look at the coconuts, cut them down, and make sure that our differences are not weaponized in the next wave of winds. Will we in fact use the wind to our advantage to continue to push the envelope for change? Let the winds of change blow, and we can collectively ride them to our end. If we harness the wind as best we can, and flow with it, the forces that would like to strong arm those that are riding these winds of change will be overrun by a new way of thinking. They will be swept up in the beauty of the diverse nature of all those who are riding the winds. They will come to realize that swinging it easy when it's breezy requires less effort, and the results are far more rewarding. God forbid, if they do not get on board with this wind, for it will surely humble them.

Chapter Eleven

"Some Days You Are the Bug, and Some Days You Are the Windshield"

At 5 a.m. one Saturday morning, I stood outside the gate of Northwest Park Golf Course. Three friends and I now golfed together every Saturday morning, and this week it was my turn to arrive right when the club opened to sign us up for the first tee time of the day. With more than 7,000 yards of fairway, Northwest Park is one of the longest public courses on the East Coast. Except for the par threes, almost every hole requires a driver. Because of the impressive grounds, you have to get there at the crack of dawn to beat the other golfers and secure one of the coveted first three tee times. Getting those tee times meant that we would be done by 10 a.m. and not take away too much time from our Saturday "Honey Do" list. At the time I had been golfing for months, and by then, I loved the game so much I was willing to do just about anything to play a round.

I also had a lot more experience under my belt. On average, I scored in the low 90's or mid-80's, so I was no longer afraid of embarrassing myself on the course. My first son was still young and Sharon and I had another child on the way, so it was still a bit challenging to fit in practice time. But I made do, often bringing my son in his stroller to the driving range to hit balls. The sport I had been so reluctant to try was now my hobby. I found golf both fun and relaxing. The game is simple (if you don't take yourself too seriously), and it provides an opportunity to enjoy the outdoors.

On this particular morning, after signing us up, I went home to try and catch a little more sleep before our tee time. On the way back to the course, one of the guys in the group called to say he wasn't going to make it. This wasn't that unusual, as every now and then one of us had to back out. Whenever this happened, the club would just bump up a single player to our tee time. I myself had been that person many times, waiting by the putting greens hoping someone ahead of me would drop out. If you were in this position, you didn't dare leave to go use the restroom or get a snack out of fear that you'd miss out.

When I pulled into the parking lot at the course, I noticed a familiar vehicle. It was a red Sterling and the license plate read "COACH." When I saw it, I did one of those double head twists like Fred Flintstone or Barney Rubble. I hadn't been able to visit Coach Moultrie on campus in a while, so I was glad to have the chance to say "hello."

I was feeling particularly confident that morning since I had been golfing decently as of late. Because my group was the first on the list, I took my time getting my golf shoes on and moseying up to the clubhouse. As I walked over, my confidence continued to bubble. That morning I felt as though I could handle the pressure of a PGA event.

When I got to the putting green for check in, I announced boldly that I was Gerald Hector and was signed up for the first tee time. My swagger was such that when I said this to the starter, I looked around at the folks who had to wait another hour or so to get off the first tee. I felt their pain. I truly did. I told the starter that a member of the group had dropped out, so we had an open spot. Internally, I really hoped that whoever they let fill our group would be able to keep up with us. We liked to move at a steady pace and finish up by 11 a.m. at the latest. Every week, we opted to walk to get our exercise instead of using a cart. Whoever joined us would just have to be OK with that. We were Saturday morning warriors and didn't like to stray from tradition.

The starter thanked me for updating him, then called out to the others gathered at the putting green. "There's been a cancellation," he said. "Moultrie, you're with the first group." Of course, I was happy to play with Coach Moultrie, but this turn of events also drained my confidence. Coach was my mentor in all things sports related, and especially since he'd seen me golf so poorly before, I felt like I had to show him how much I'd improved. I needed to prove to Coach that I had better control of my shots and had learned the cardinal rules of golf since I'd last played with him. In my head, I went over these principles to prepare for the game; *Drive for show, putt for dough, never leave the birdie putt short, at all costs avoid the indignity of having your drive stop short of the lady's tee box.* I felt confident that I'd get through the course without making any of these mistakes. After all, I'd put in enough practice.

When I spotted Coach Moultrie, I walked over and greeted him. In his distinct, booming voice he said he had suspected it was me when he saw the name Hector atop the list. I told Coach that my group was accustomed to walking the course, but I fully expected him to grab a cart for himself. To my surprise, he decided to join us in our quest for exercise. *Lord have mercy,* I thought to myself, impressed that Coach wanted to spend the whole morning on his feet. He was by no means ancient, but you wouldn't expect a man of his age to be interested in walking all 18 holes while lugging around a heavy set of clubs.

I'm not sure if there really was a crowd or if I only imagined it, but it felt like everyone was watching our little group as we set up at the starting tee. Suddenly, I felt an invisible weight hanging around my shoulders. The other guys at the course knew me well and knew that Coach Moultrie had been my track coach in college. I knew they would view this entire round of golf as a competition between the two of us.

As we did every week, we had a tee toss in the air to see who would go first. As luck or fate would have it, I ended up hitting last. My friend Bevin went first. He was a retired businessman I met at Northwest Park one Saturday morning. We'd both signed up as single players that weekend and were put in the same group. For the first nine holes, we said nothing to one another. We just played. Then, at the 10th hole, he missed a short two-foot putt and to my surprise, he swore to himself in the same melodic tone that all Jamaican's have in common. Lightly put, let us just say his words of disappointment stitched several pieces of cloth together. I was overjoyed to have met another *"yaad man"* who loved golf. After that moment, we relaxed around each other and talked during the rest of the round. We discussed politics, music, and everything in between. Bevin was a good dude and that day was the start of a friendship around the sport of golf.

My other friend, Michael, was up next. He is full Jamaican and an accomplished track and field official as well. He had become a real staple at the annual Penn Relays. He never let his patois lapse-it was always in full bloom and full flight. I liked that about him. He was an unashamed *"yaad man"* through and through.

Both Bevin and Michael made good distance and their shots went straight down the middle. Then, it was Coach Moultrie's turn. In typical Coach Moultrie fashion, he whistled as he approached the tee box. Just like that day at Needwood, he didn't speak much other than whispering encouragements to himself. "Now come on you puppy," he said. "Let's go." The Ti Bubble Burner screamed with his drive. With a nice roll, the ball went right down the middle. People watching clapped and whistled and just like that, the pressure was on.

As I stepped up to the tee, the small crowd suddenly became reminiscent of an audience at the first hole of Pebble Beach. All three men ahead of me had made perfect drives, and there I was with sweaty palms unsure I'd get anywhere close to the greens, particularly since the first hole was reachable for long hitters. I felt the old urge to just muscle the ball as hard as I could. I also felt the sudden urge to puke. The longer I waited to swing, the more my confidence waned. "Shake it off," I said to myself. "Be a man." (in my best Martin Lawrence voice).

I regrouped and stepped closer. My set up was good and I had my spine angled just right. I took a few practice swings to make sure I could transfer my weight smoothly. My head was behind the ball and I had everything lined up perfectly just like I'd done on many Saturday mornings. The practice swings I'd taken were so flawless they barely brushed the grass or disturbed the morning dew.

157

With my head down, I finally took my actual swing. But unlike my practice swings, nothing went quite right. I caught just a glimpse of my ball in flight, and things were not looking good. Bevin confirmed this when he said, *"A wah dat? A which part the ball a guh?"*

I looked over at Coach Moultrie, dreading his reaction to my terrible shot. But he didn't acknowledge it. He just continued to whistle to himself, grabbed his bag, and started down the fairway. I made the conscious decision not to look back at the crowd that was watching from the practice green, but I did hear someone utter *"rhatid,"* which is patois for hell. Feeling dejected, I set off after Coach Moultrie toward the next tee.

With par on the next few holes, I was able to somewhat correct the round. Slowly, my wheels came off the ground. I felt like I was about to soar. The driver started behaving for me and I was hitting roughly 280 yards. But I would then miss the green or be so far from the hole on the approach shot that no putt was within 20 feet. Only a few of my approach shots were on in regulation. I had so many three-putt bogies that day that it almost drove me to drink. Meanwhile, Coach kept whistling and remained as steady as they come. He hit fairways and second shots into the green in regulation. Bevin and Michael had well-controlled games as well.

I was playing a working man's round, keeping it respectable. I was behind, but not embarrassingly so. Everything was going OK, but on the back nine, I broke the last basic principle of golf that I was so sure I wouldn't mess up. At the 11th hole, I rose up out of my swing too quickly and topped the ball with my driver.

Bevin, Michael, Coach Moultrie, and I watched as the ball moved in agonizingly slow motion and trickled toward the female tee box. Meanwhile, I silently tried to plead my case to God for a miracle that would keep the ball rolling just a couple more feet. But my plea went unanswered. The ball stopped just short of the women's tee box.

I knew Coach Moultrie would have nothing to say while we were still on the course, so I waited for Bevin and Michael to chime in. True to form, Michael spoke up. *"You know wah suppose to happen yah now? But since a di first time wi si you a do dat wi ago ease yuh up."* Their laughter was not only boisterous but piercing. I was about ready to call it a day. As I looked over at Coach, I knew he understood Michael's every word, and the penalty for such a sorry shot was universally known. Humiliated, I headed towards my ball to prep for my second shot.

Fortunately, I redeemed myself in the remainder of the round. I birdied the long, par-five 17th hole and also got a par on the final hole going back up the hill. No surprise, Coach Moultrie ended up with the lowest score and Bevin and Michael both finished ahead of me. To my relief, my score was within my usual range despite my rather embarrassing mistakes. But regardless, those botched shots haunted me as we walked back towards the clubhouse.

After a gentleman's handshake, we headed back to our cars, Coach Moultrie and I walking side by side. Now that the round was over, I knew he'd have something to say to me, and I dreaded his critique. Still in silence, we knocked the grass off our shoes and wiped off our clubs. True to form, Coach finally spoke up.

"Hector, your game has improved," he said. "You drove the ball well at times, but you need to learn to read the greens better and to release the putter when you putt. You can't stab at the ball and think it's going to stay on line. The putter should swing like a pendulum. Just keep practicing Son. You will play this game for life." I responded that I wished I had more time to practice, and Coach replied: "We all do Son. But here's another bit of advice for you. You have to remember that some days you will be the bug and some days you will be the windshield."

"What do you mean, Coach?" I asked. "Hector," he said. "You've seen the pros play. They don't have time to dwell on bad shots. They regroup instantly and move on to the next hole. You're no pro, but still, rehearsing the bad shot in your mind over and over takes away the focus you need for the next hole. After you topped that ball on the 11th hole, you lost your concentration. You were killing the ball for most of the round on the driver, but you missed the birdie putt on 10 and you took that with you to the tee on 11. Your friends told you they'd watch your ball, so what were you doing lifting your head up so soon on that drive? It's a mental game Son. You will have good and bad days. You'll always have a chance on the next hole or the next round. Both in this game of golf, and in life."

I looked at Coach and nodded in agreement. There I was, years after graduating Howard, still getting life coaching from Coach Moultrie. Like always, he gave me the exact advice I needed. Every day since that conversation, I've tried to heed those words, not only on the greens, but in my career, relationships, and personal pursuits.

But compared to golf, managing a career and a family isn't so cut and dry. There are some days that I get splattered on the windshield. But thank God, there are more days when I am the windshield blocking the bugs. I've found that what is most important is how you recover. How do you get back up again when life takes an unexpected turn? It is during those times that your true character shows. In terms of the star apple tree, the fruit I gained from Coach Moultrie's advice that day at the golf course was perspective.

Ithaca, New York where I lived isn't very far from the city of Corning. Corning is home to the Corning Glass Works, a famous glassware company. The city also has the Corning Museum of Glass, a museum entirely dedicated to glass and the process of glass blowing. When I moved to Upstate New York, I had very little interest in visiting the museum. After all, it's just glass. Who out there has a passion for glass? But I didn't want to repeat the same mistake I'd made while living in Washington D.C. When I was there, I never made the time to visit all the museums and monuments, and now I regret it. I did the same thing when I lived in Charlotte by never hiking Blue Ridge Mountain. This time, I wanted to be a bit more cultured and see what the region had to offer.

In awe of the glass making process I did not listen intently during the tour, but when I got home, I researched and pieced most of the process together. Now, I won't bore you with the details. Instead, I'll just give you a sense of what my research revealed...I learned that glass is made from liquid sand. Growing up going to Jamaican beaches, I thought I understood just how hot sand could get, but that was nothing compared to this. To liquify the sand and make glass, they heat it up to over 3,000 degrees Fahrenheit. When sand is molten and begins to cool, it turns into an amorphous solid that can be manipulated into whatever you want it to be. But the molten sand still needs to be enhanced. During the heating and melting phase, glass makers add limestone and soda ash to the sand. The soda ash reduces the sand's melting point then limestone is added so the glass won't dissolve in water. The final result is the hardened glass we use for common objects.

Like Coach Moultrie said, some days, we are the windshield. We are a surface that is hardened and smooth because of what we have gone through. We've undergone a transformation that required heat, pressure, twisting, and turning. We've all been broken down then later built back up becoming something new.

There are a lot of processes like this. For example, in the Bible, the Book of 1st Peter tells us about being placed in a crucible and having to endure heat and pressure in order to remove impurities and come out as pure gold. Diamonds are formed via a similar process. A lump of coal is placed under immense pressure then eventually becomes a perfect diamond. Or, for good measure, we can refer to lumps of clay placed on a potter's wheel. The potter molds and shapes the clay by hand, but for that pot or vessel to be of any use, it will first have to go into the kiln's fire. All these examples share the same basic principle: creating a product that has value, the original must first be shaped and hardened.

What concerns me is that we aren't always committed to this process. We lack the proper perspective to realize that life's challenges help to strengthen us. In other words, we aren't willing to go through the necessary process to become whatever we are destined to be. I recently adopted the following saying I heard from Congressman Elijah Cummings: "When you notice things in life are happening all around you, the question is not why is this happening to you, but more importantly why is this happening for you?" (paraphrased). Our perspective is key.

An easy way to understand this is through the lens of parenting. As previously mentioned, I coached soccer during the years my kids played. I'm sure you've probably heard of helicopter parents. They're the ones who constantly dote on their children and never let them grow up and become independent. Then, there are the soccer parents who just want to see their kids get some playing time and receive a participation trophy at the end of the season, simply because they tried. Today, we also encounter lawnmower parents. These parents will do anything to make sure their children never experience any form of hardship. I frequently met this sort of parent while I was coaching soccer for my children at the youth level. I once heard a mom explaining to other moms why she thought this was the best way to raise her kids. It was none of my business, so I stayed out of it. Though I swear my mouth was bleeding because of how hard I had to bite my tongue. As I listened, something Coach Moultrie once said to me came to mind: "They don't make them like they used to. We have all these Similac babies running around."

While the soccer moms and dads continued chatting, I thought to myself: what happens when their kids become teenagers and adults? Eventually, they'll have to face some sort of adversity. We live in a world filled with hardship and heartbreak. Sadly, children are currently growing up in an era where opioid addiction and suicide are increasing at alarming rates. I firmly believe that hiding children from reality ultimately does them more harm than good. I am no psychologist, but this is a phenomenon I find intriguing. But this doesn't just apply to children, we will each face a measure of adversity throughout our lives.

The truth is, we all must go through a few fires to come out refined on the other side. Many times, we do not discover our strength until we are tested. It's when we are just about to throw in the towel or when we start to lose our religion that we experience real growth. Especially if you want to become a leader, you will face trials that push you right to the edge. I won't sugarcoat the truth: most leaders rise to their positions because they have learned from being used, misunderstood, betrayed, lied on, and ostracized. The level of severity might be a little different in each case, but they each experienced a proving ground.

The good thing is, life typically throws us some limestone or soda ash along the way to help us become the final product. For example, I have had mentors in my life like Coach Moultrie, who have helped me through the process with their time, talent, and treasure. These people are sounding boards and advocates. I've had people like this at every stage of my life. In preparatory school at Our Lady of the Angels, I had Sister Shirley. In high school at Kingston College, I had Mr. Bruce Bryan and Reverend JAH Ramsey. Just thinking of them warms my heart, despite the fact that at times they practiced tough love. They were the ones who administered "canings" for being recalcitrant in getting assignments done on time in high school. They were a part of the crucible that as a young man I had to go through to come out refined and prepared for the world. Over the years, I've had numerous coaches who pushed me to my limits to help me become a better student-athlete. There was George Thompson, Roy McClean, Gladstone Neil, Mabricio Ventura Sr., Duke Fuller, Mr. Youngster Goldsmith, and a host of others.

During my college career, there was William Moultrie (obviously), Barron Harvey, and Frank Ross. In my professional career I had Christopher Nicholson, William H. Gray III, Dorothy Yancy, MaryLou Merkt, and recently, Lynne Schafer. For spiritual guidance, my wife Sharon-Kaye is the anchor. Bishop Claude Richard Alexander, Cynthia Maxwell, Eric Reed, Avis Graves, Michael Dean Perry, and Richard Nichols have also made significant contributions in keeping me grounded and focused through music, words, and deeds.

All these people come to mind because they made deposits in my life and career at exactly the right moment. I have lived in three countries and three states within the United States, and in each place, I've met people who challenged me and kept me grounded. At times, I did not want to speak to them because I knew I had either messed up or simply did not want to be bothered listening to them. But there were just as many times when I ran to them for the soothing ministry they provided or for guidance regarding what was next for me. To this day some of them don't realize how much they've helped me, and probably would be shocked that they are even mentioned here.

On the other hand, there were times where someone's disloyalty and betrayal also taught me a lesson. I won't get into the details, but this has happened to me several times throughout my career. I once hired an individual who I thought was fit for a particular job, but later discovered that all he cared about was power. By working for me, he was that much closer to the top of the executive food chain. By hiring him, I put my reputation on the line. Soon, undermining me became the order of the day, and I learned that colleagues I'd trusted were challenged by my rapid rise within the organization. That's when I knew it was time to make a move. As soon as a trusted leader retired, I promptly moved on. Thankfully, I had spiritual mentors who gave me good counsel during this trial. They quoted Scripture to me and encouraged me to let the Lord fight my battles. At the same time, I had my "street advisors," my friends who told me to fight fire with fire. Conflicted no doubt, but I chose the former over the latter.

In the end, I was able to keep my head on my shoulders. I decided to sit still and watch God do His work. This turned out to be the best decision I could have made. Not only was I removed from the situation, but my career was elevated. The person I'd hired was eventually burned by his own ego. Attempts to reengage have been ignored. Coach Moultrie always said, "The first time the dog bites you. It's the dog's fault. The second time the dog bites you, it's your fault." I was not going to get bitten twice.

Things like this have happened several times since. But with each instance, I had a bit more experience and knew how to handle the situation. That's not to say it always worked out the way I wanted, but still, through these challenges, my character was hardening and taking shape. I became battle tested, and now I can see such things coming from a mile away.

I share these stories because they are situations in which no lawnmower or helicopter parent could have come and saved me from. It's good to have mentors, but ultimately, they can't walk in your shoes. You must face your challenges yourself. If I had not gone through iterations of disappointment and gotten my childish tendencies and reactions out of my system, I would not have matured and become self-sufficient, wiser, and more discerning of every situation I encounter. Without the hardening process, I would still be in an amorphous state troubled by everything that anyone said to me. Responding to everything and everyone is not productive when what is required is simply an exhibition of quiet confidence.

I've grown older and years wrought with challenges have hardened me. Nowadays, I have way more good days than bad. Things tend to bounce off me a bit more. The winds that would once have obstructed my vision and distracted me from my goals no longer bother me. The hardened glass of my windshield blocks the wind. I may never be bulletproof, but I am far better protected than I would be had I never faced adversity.

Over the years, I've changed my perspective on the hardships in life. When a challenge arises, I now know that I can handle it. Because I've faced trials before, I know what works and what doesn't. I try to simply trust the process and let go of the things that are bigger than me.

While living in Ithaca, at least once a month, Sharon and I drove down to Washington D.C. We always had a good time hanging out with friends and living it up in a big city. While living in Ithaca, we missed metropolitan life terribly. I've lived in three places since coming to the United States, but Sharon and I will always consider D.C. our home base. It's where Howard is, and where many of our friends stayed following graduation.

Whenever Sharon and I visited D.C., we tried to stretch our stay for as long as we could. We often didn't leave the city until Sunday evening, though it's a long drive back to Ithaca. Consequently, we'd often end up driving home in the dark. Pennsylvania is quite scenic in the daylight, especially in the fall when the leaves change colors, but at night, it's a dark place with long stretches of highway without streetlights, forcing you to rely solely on your headlights. If you aren't accustomed to driving at night, the trip can be daunting.

One drive home in particular, I was reminded of what Coach Moultrie said: "Some days you will be the bug and sometimes you will be the windshield." Before we left D.C., I washed the car. It looked spic and span and I even paid an extra dollar to have Rain-X applied. The windshield was spotless. We stopped at a friend's house then hit the road around 5 p.m. If we made good time, we'd be back in Ithaca around midnight. It was still daylight when we started up I-270, but the sun had started to fade by the time we hit Harrisburg. When we

168

reached Lewistown, it was completely dark. But all was well; we had a full tank of gas, our iPods loaded with music, and each other for company. I had Sharon to talk with at the start of the trip, but soon, she drifted off to sleep.

We were about four hours into the drive home when I noticed several specs on the windshield. To clear them, I turned on the washer and wipers. I instantly realized that was a mistake. Whatever the specs were, the wipers dragged them across the entire windshield leaving behind a nasty residue. Wondering what I was up against, I turned on my high beams. It turns out, I was driving through a giant swarm of insects. They hit my windshield in rapid succession, which continued for at least 10 minutes. But finally, the bugs cleared, and I had a peaceful drive the rest of the way. We arrived home a little past midnight and headed straight to bed.

Early the next morning, I got up, dressed, and headed out the door for work. Still perturbed about the bugs on my windshield, I wanted to see if I could clean off their remains before I left for work. To my surprise, not only was the windshield caked with bug juice, but the hood, front grill, and the back of the rear-view mirrors were covered as well. I immediately headed out to a self-service car wash.

As I scraped bug guts off my car, I couldn't help but feel a bit bad for the little fellows. They were so tiny compared to my massive vehicle which came at them at 70 miles per hour. Remembering Coach Moultrie's comment, I started thinking about all the times in my life that I had been blindsided and knocked down. Just like those little bugs on the windshield, I've had my fair share of accidents. Fortunately, I've been able to get back up each time.

But learning from accidents, mistakes, and failures is easier said than done. Sometimes, these incidents throw us back into a conservative mindset. Out of fear, we don't want to jump back into whatever it was we failed at. We get stuck remembering the pain or embarrassment of the incident and it prevents us from trying again. Or, we get stuck in over analysis trying to figure out exactly where we may have gone wrong.

Though we may not call it imposter syndrome, we all face situations in life that knock us off our feet and cause us to second-guess ourselves. Truly, this happens to everyone at one time or another. I have friends who are pastors and they've told me that after preaching a sermon, they've sometimes fallen into a depressive state. Once they've delivered their message, they start dissecting everything they said. Not only that, they start questioning their own motivations or try to gauge how the congregation responded. This fact blew my mind a bit to know that even pastors experience self-doubt.

How do you recuperate from failure or get past self-doubt? I think the solution is simple: we need to stop taking everything so seriously. The truth is, people fail. And yes, failure hurts, but it isn't permanent, and it isn't always our own shortcomings that knock us down. Sometimes, it's other people. I've found that especially in the workplace, people lash out because of jealousy, causing others to stumble. Hurting people, hurt people. An interesting meme I saw recently asserted: "If you don't heal from what hurt you the last time, you will

bleed on others you come in contact with next time."
Too many times we don't truly heal before jumping into
the next situation.

In truth, life can sometimes feel like one accident
after another. One day, something happens at work that
makes you look bad in front of your boss. The next day,
your kid does something awful and it makes you feel
like you've failed as a parent. The day after that, you
find out that your parents are sick and need care. We've
all experienced trials and had to decide what to do
when hardship arises.

It's in these very moments that we need proper
perspective. When you make a mistake or tragedy
strikes, that is when you have to remember that you've
been down that road before and survived. You've
learned from your experiences. You have overcome
your imposter syndrome in the past, and you can do it
again.

I experienced this principle at work when Coach
Moultrie had a stroke and I went to visit him at the
Washington Hospital Center. While there, we had a
conversation regarding people and how they tend to
react too strongly to their circumstances. According to
Coach, if you live your life that way and never step back
to view your situation with the proper perspective, you
will simply flail about in the wind. Here was a man I had
a tremendous amount of respect for, who had taught me
so much about living in the United States as a youngster,
who by all indications was a healthy man yet had a
stroke. While in this state, his mind and wit did not
diminish. He said to me, "Son, old coach has had a
setback. The body failed me, but my mind is still intact."

He still wanted to operate as if he had not had this setback. My teammate Shaun Bell tells the story of when Coach asked him to get him out of the bed despite the nurses' instructions. We all laugh at that story because that was Coach. He was not going to let anything get him down.

For years he was the windshield that we all viewed as our protector, advisor, advocate, mentor, father figure, and friend. All of a sudden, he was now the bug. However, the remarkable fortitude that Coach exhibited during that setback made it hard to tell that he was the bug. He would not allow it. That is how I strive to be today. He used to tell us, "Never let them see you sweat Son. When they see you sweat, is when they've got you." I used that approach recently with an individual, and the person's response was, "You are not even fighting or pushing back?" In that conversation I had already decided not to let any emotions become evident because I was *playing di fool fi ketch di wise.* My mind was already made up as to what I was going to do, and those plans did not include that individual or any derivatives from the situation. It works, and the peace it brings is indescribable. I have come to process that approach in the context of knowing exactly when I am the bug, and what my reaction and approach is going to be, versus when I am the windshield and how I will treat people. The two are mutually exclusive, but in the cadence of life, they are inextricably linked.

Chapter Twelve

"Run Here or Run Away from Here"

The ballroom of the Blackburn Center, which sits right at the heart of the Howard University campus, had been immaculately prepared. Round tables that seat 10 people each were strategically placed around the room. The place settings were first-class, the décor glistened. The waitstaff stood off to the corners, dressed in their finest threads.

Whenever Howard University puts on a formal event, they do it with class. The annual athletic banquets I attended were no exception. Every year, all of us student-athletes dressed to the nines for a special dinner in our honor. Both the men's and women's teams came together for a night of camaraderie and celebration. It was always a beautiful sight to see.

Personally, I liked being surrounded by people who, like me, were at Howard with a one-shot dream. A lot of us were on a similar journey, evidenced by the way we dressed. The event was very formal, but because we came from various socioeconomic backgrounds, we wore what we had. I'd say the majority of the athletes at the banquet wore mixed-matched pieces, but we were "clean" nonetheless.

I was curious to see what Coach Moultrie would show up wearing. He did not disappoint. When he entered the ballroom, he immediately removed his wide-brimmed hat. He wore his signature Texan cowboy boots and a suit with razor sharp seams. (Seriously, if someone got too close, they would have been sliced.) I won't say he was the best dressed coach at the banquet, but he certainly set the atmosphere for the event. His appearance, coupled with the way he walked, set a fine example. He exuded confidence and gravitas.

I remember my freshman year banquet very clearly. People made speeches, coaches handed out awards, and we all enjoyed an excellent meal. At every table heartfelt laughter and genuine conversation was heard. The whole athletic department resembled one big family. Not a single person was left out of the fun. Obviously, not everyone received an athletic or academic award, nevertheless, everyone in the room heavily applauded each award that was handed out over the course of the evening.

By the end of the event, I was feeling quite sappy. In my typical sentimental fashion, I walked over to Coach Moultrie to express my gratitude and pride. And, per my usual, I had prepared an entire speech. "Coach," I said. "I just wanted to stop by your table before the banquet ended to simply say thank you. Thank you for believing in me and for giving me a chance to be a Howard Bison. Even better, a Howard Track Bison. This event has been spectacular," I continued. "I never experienced anything like this. I have attended team events growing up, but not a formal banquet where I received an award. I feel a true sense of belonging on this campus right now. But I wish everyone could have received some kind of award. I know everyone seemed happy all evening, but I know the individuals who didn't get an award must feel somewhat left out."

I knew my comment had prompted a teaching moment when Coach asked me to sit down and talk. But unlike most of the lessons I'd experienced with Coach in his office, this one was straight forward. "Son," he said. "What does the sign on my office door read?" I had to pause and think about it. I'd been to Coach's office a few times during my freshman year, but he had a literal open-door policy, so I rarely ever saw the sign, because its tattered posting was on his office door. "Was it something about running?" I replied. "You should have it emblazoned on the frontal lobe of your brain," said Coach. "It's simple. It says, 'you either run here, or run away from here.' What do you think that means, Son?" After thinking for a minute, I responded: "It means that you either run fast or leave." In my mind, I was equating running with my duties as a full-scholarship athlete and all the things I had to accomplish on the track to maintain that scholarship. Lord knows that if I'd lost any portion of my funding, there would've been no way I could graduate.

"You are half right," said Coach Moultrie. "But I want you to fully understand and appreciate the statement. Howard University creates leaders. The place has an ethos of excellence. Within the track and field program, we expect excellence at all times and in all places. That includes what happens on the track, in the field, in the residence halls, in the cafeteria, and out amongst the general public."

As Coach continued, he looked directly at me, giving me that familiar feeling that he was peering straight into my soul. "Remember those T-shirts I had printed? The ones that read, 'Not everyone can be a Track Bison?' The shirts were meant to make a public

175

statement. When you wear the shirt, you're not just representing yourself, you're representing this program and this prestigious university. Howard University athletics represents excellence. Not just on the track or field, but in your classes and reflected in your GPA. Hector, think about how many track athletes won academic awards tonight. Yes, I care about your performance as an athlete, but I'm more concerned about your academic achievements. This program isn't just about sports, Son. It's about life."

I understood what Coach was saying; the track team consisted of a truly special group of people who thrived both athletically and academically. I was extremely proud of that. But I still didn't see the connection between this and the sign on his door. Like clockwork, Coach interrupted my thoughts with the answer to my question. "With that said, Son, the folks who didn't receive an award tonight have some work to do. If they haven't fully bought into the notion of excellence, then this might not be the place or program for them. Eventually, these individuals will self-select. They'll stop trying at practices then stop showing up altogether. Then they'll officially quit the program. They might even leave the university."

For a second, Coach's statements sounded harsh to me. But he continued: "Hector, always remember that excellence comes at a cost. If you aren't happy with your prescribed course of action in anything you attempt, you have options. You should always enjoy the environment in which you are learning, growing, and developing. It's all about finding where you fit. If you don't truly belong to a group or a process and you try to force yourself into it, you'll only be wasting your time.

Instead of spending all this energy trying to bend an entire process or organization to suit you, you should look for a setting where you are comfortable and can truly grow."

When Coach said this, I thought about the students in the athletic department who were half-stepping. These were those who were on the rosters but not really on their teams mentally. They complained a lot. They always had some issue going on that distracted them. This was the type of student-athlete Coach referred to as a dormitory lawyer. They were always looking for shortcuts. Looking back now, I recognize that these were in fact the very team members who eventually quit their programs for various reasons.

After the banquet, I rarely passed Coach's office again without thinking about that sign on the door. The words became a mantra for me, and they've stayed with me as I navigate my way through my career. Over the years, I've remembered this sign every time I started to feel out of place in any situation, especially when lived experiences suggest that the situation would not end well. It is in those moments that we get our greatest clarity. Having mentors and advisors who have experienced these issues before who can assist us is a huge bonus. A "kitchen cabinet" of mentors is an invaluable asset.

I try to live my life with the assertion that I either run there or run away from there. I have been in environments where I was unhappy and risked simply going through the motions. That is not a part of my DNA. I always want to be contributing at a level, where I believe I am having an impact. If I find myself having responsibility but no authority, now because of my lived experiences, I realize I have options to consider.

It is no one else's responsibility to make you happy or productive in whatever you do in this life. You must do this for yourself. For me, I've found the book *Experiencing God* by Henry Blackaby to be extremely helpful. In his book, Blackaby discusses seven truths you should consider during any decision-making process around one's spirituality:

1. God is always at work around you.

2. God pursues a continuous relationship of love with you that is real and personal.

3. God invites you to become involved with Him and His work.

4. God speaks through the Holy Spirit, the Bible, prayer, circumstances, and the church to reveal Himself, His purpose, and His ways.

5. God's invitation to work with Him always leads to a crisis of belief that requires faith and action.

6. You must make major adjustments in your life to join God in what He is doing.

7. You come to know God through experiences as you obey Him and He accomplishes His work through you.

These seven tenets are spiritual, but I believe they mirror the message Coach Moultrie was trying to convey to me at the banquet. The decision to embrace the excellence of Howard University was a conscious one. As students, coaches, professors, teammates, and colleagues, we all had to ensure that we were fully attuned to what was expected of us as members of the Bison family.

Using Blackaby's seven steps to Experiencing God as a base, this is what I believe every Howard Bison must understand and embrace:

1. There is always work to be done. Every time you show up for a task, you must give an honest effort.

2. Your professors, coaches, teammates, and those who care about you will always try to find ways to encourage you as you matriculate. At Howard, everyone is in it together.

3. At Howard, you will be invited to live, learn, and leave your comfort zone. You'll have to jump into situations and circumstances that are foreign to you, and you're better off taking this leap than playing it safe. It's when you are uncomfortable and frustrated that your inner creativity and desire for more kick in.

4. The challenging circumstances you face at Howard will only make you stronger, wiser, and better. Experience strengthens the character traits that lay dormant within you. You will need these traits to move on to the next level of your life and career. Furthermore, you'll need them to face any difficult situation you're bound to

179

encounter.

5. You will feel the *Imposter Syndrome*. You're being educated at one of the most prestigious universities in the world, but that doesn't exempt you from the discrimination and implicit bias you will face because of your black skin. You'll have to work through this and believe that you belong, that you will succeed, and exceed all expectations-even your own.

6. What you learned prior to attending Howard may be a good foundation, but you'll have to start building yet again to shape what comes next. You'll have to sacrifice four years of your life for the rest of your life.

7. Success isn't defined by the material things you acquire but by the lasting impact you leave on the world. The formation of Howard University was for the "least of these," and Howard graduates have excelled in all fields and gone on to influence global change. As a Howard student, your experiences and achievements are pivotal for every "What's Next?" in the world...

Prior to my arrival at Howard University, I'd had several coaches in Jamaica. The majority of my formative years were spent there, with the exception of two years spent in Trinidad and Tobago. Therefore, it is safe to say that all my mannerisms, sense of fair play, justice, and community came from my time growing up in that little island paradise. It is on that beautiful island that my love for sports grew exponentially. If it was soccer, I idolized Pele of Brazil. Tottenham Hotspurs was and continues to be my favorite team in the English Premier League. I was drawn to the personalities of Garth Crooks, Ricky Kempes, Glenn Hoddle, and Osvaldo Ardilles (the little Argentinian magician). Why I am still a fan warrants another book. If it was cricket, I was drawn to the greats of the West Indies. There are too many to mention, but let's just say, all the players who I was able to skip school at Kingston College to watch play at Sabina Park were my favorites. In track and field, there were many; Herbert McKinley, Mabricio Ventura, Milton Smith, and all the other elder statesmen of Kingston College's glorious competitive spirit against archrival Calabar during the 80's. I count even the fights off the field amongst supporters as part of the culture surrounding competition.

It is with this background that I came to the United States. I had coaches in all three sports. They each had their own philosophies on how the sport was to be played. I am thankful to this day, that I had coaches who progressively established firm foundations in my local communities.

Skills in all three sports were honed in the dustbowls of Edgewater and Garveymeade for soccer. Mentors/coaches like Rollin Mercurious, Hopeton "Jack" Francis, and Roy "Son Son" Cobrey were instrumental in developing my love for soccer. Once I got to high school, the love for the game kept me going until I finally ended up playing in the Manning Cup for the legendary George Thompson.

In cricket, the same route was noticeable. I played cork and tar cricket on the asphalt roads of

Garveymeade where pace bowling on the uneven asphalt might send you to the hospital that very day; however, that did not take away from me having to learn how to bowl a ball on the proper length. Bat Up and Ketch, and Golf Cricket were second to none. I moved through the ranks to finally play cricket for the legendary Roy McClean at the Sunlight and Tappin Cup levels at Kingston College. When I lived in Trinidad and Tobago, we secured the first ever regional cricket title for St. Josephs College, a private religiously affiliated high school. Getting involved in track and field was simply a product of having untapped energy and good leg speed. Now that I am wiser, I can't help but think that I probably should have spent more time learning how to run properly. Who knows what might have become of it? I was what some of my friends call a "dry foot" specialist.

Back to Coach's advice that night at the athletic banquet, coupled with weaving my youthful athletic career with his words brought about a common thread of thought. You have to be happy doing what you are called to do because that happiness will bring with it a commitment that no one can teach.

Interestingly, I now serve on the board of trustees for the Gordon Conwell Theological Seminary. At each board meeting, we share dinner where the trustees and faculty get together to break bread. We also end up having great conversations about all sorts of topics.

During one such meeting, I had the occasion of speaking with Professor Pablo Polischuk. We were talking about a wide range of topics, one of which was his work in establishing a non-denominational seminary in his homeland of Argentina. As the discussion progressed, he cited an old cliché often used amongst leaders that goes something like this: "You can lead a horse to water, but you cannot make it drink." His resulting play on words stuck with me because it reminded me of the words Coach Moultrie shared with me in the spring of 1990 at the annual athletic banquet. He said, "If there is a little bit of salt in a horse's mouth when you lead it to water, it will want to drink." At the time I laughed heartily, however, in my quiet time as I drifted off to sleep that night, his play on words resonated with me.

Coach Moultrie was subtly telling me during our conversation at the banquet that Howard University was giving me the salt necessary for me to be successful. That salt would cause me to be thirsty, and want to quench that thirst. He let me know in his own way that this thirst could only be quenched through new knowledge, new experiences, new growth, and new development. On the other hand, inflexibility, and working within any scenario that does not bring about a sense of inquisitiveness and happiness would be detrimental. Any of us finding ourselves in a stagnant situation would eventually come to a decision point, that left unanswered, would cause us to languish in a familiar quagmire of mediocrity.

One of the saddest things I've observed over the years is people who remain in jobs, relationships and situations where they are unhappy. Because they lack the will or courage to make changes, they have resigned themselves to becoming complacent in this thing called life.

Maybe, just maybe, Coach's words should be a reminder to us all. If we can't run where we are currently located or situated, maybe we should run from there and strive to make the impact we are each destined to leave on this earth...

About the Author

Gerald L. Hector, CPA currently serves as the Executive Vice President and Chief Business Officer for Morehouse College in Atlanta, Georgia. He oversees all the business and finance activities of the college, and has responsibility for the following units: Finance, Budget and Planning, Auxiliary Services, Facilities, Information Technology, Human Resources, Campus Operations and Treasury. He joined Morehouse in May of 2019.

Prior to Morehouse College, he served as the Vice President for Financial Affairs and Treasurer at Cornell University, one of the nation's eight Ivy League schools. At Cornell he oversaw all finance, procurement, treasury (including debt management), policy, tax, risk management, and sponsored financial services (post award). In his role he was responsible for a debt portfolio of $1.3 billion, and also responsible for the financial reporting of this organization with an annual budget of $4.5 billion.

He also served as the Vice President of Finance and Administration at Ithaca College, Vice President for Business and Finance at Johnson C. Smith University, and the Corporate Controller for the United Negro College Fund. While at the United Negro College Fund under the leadership of William H. Gray, III he was afforded the opportunity to become part of a team that created the initial budgets and financial operations of the Gates Millennium Scholars Program. It was a $1 billion scholarship program established by the Bill and Melinda Gates Foundation for the purpose of educating 20 thousand minority students. Established in 1998, the program is on target to meet and exceed its expectations.

In addition to his formal work within institutions of higher education, he is an avid supporter of HBCUs (Historically Black Colleges and Universities). Being a Howard University graduate, that was a simple symbiotic relationship, and one that he cherishes in terms of giving back to HBCUs as they navigate these challenging times. His landmark paper: "Navigating the New Normal: Financial Imperatives for MSI Effectiveness and Avoiding Financial Exigency" is a must read for trustees of small to medium sized higher education institutions. He has presented at several conferences and facilitated several board retreats for institutions across the nation.

Hailing from Kingston, Jamaica, he earned an athletic scholarship to Howard University where he graduated with honors within four years. Although he has written white papers and articles for the higher education industry, this is his first book to say "thank you" to his university coach: William P. Moultrie, but he has also has a second book in the works which focuses on the pending changes in higher education from the perspective of a senior administration official of several institutions.

He is married to Sharon-Kaye Hector (nee Smith), and their union has produced three children: Joshua, Timothy and Kezia. He is an avid reader, sports enthusiast, and golfer. He continues to speak on the public circuit, which includes two HBCU's one medium-sized PWI, and one of the nation's eight Ivy League institutions. Gerald Hector is highly sought-after regarding matters of HCBU's and higher education in general.

More on William P. Moultrie

When I entered Howard University as a freshman, Coach Moultrie knew that I wanted to pursue a career in science. Howard students respected "The Valley", as it was called, where all the science courses were taught. Coach Moultrie always told me..."*You are going to have to work hard, love God, and be twice as good to get out of here.*" He was absolutely right, and I have applied that philosophy to every aspect of my career in Clinical Research.

---Tamecia Williams, MS
Assoc. Director, Clinical Operations
IQVIA

Listen to advice and accept instruction, that you may gain wisdom in the future. Proverbs 19:20

I came home from school one afternoon to find Coach Moultrie sitting in my scantily furnished living room, talking to my mother. I was a hardheaded, poor kid with attitude living in the inner city of Baltimore, and here he was going on about an opportunity for me to attend Howard University. It turned out to be the day that changed my life!

Coach gave his spiel which didn't sound much different than what any other coach would say to a recruit. Then Coach Moultrie said, "Hell Felder, you're a thoroughbred and you need to be at Howard. A degree from 'The Mecca' will change your life!"

That really resonated with me. During the recruiting process, every coach talked about how much better of a sprinter I would become under their program. They talked about the records I could break and running accolades that I could achieve. That all sounded pretty good to me. No other coach talked about me obtaining a degree or about the experience changing my life. I listened to Coach Moultrie's words. It wasn't just what he said, but how he said it. I believed in him. My mom believed in him. After that my destiny was decided and it was the absolute best decision I've ever made!

I don't believe I'd be the woman I am today had our paths not crossed. Coach Moultrie taught me to be humble rather than boastful. He taught me how to be patient and adaptable. He taught me how to persevere during difficult times. He taught me that it was alright to be vulnerable, as long as I picked myself up by the bootstraps. Most importantly, he taught me that I needed to help myself in order to be able to help others!

Coach and I have had countless conversations over the years. He was the first person I always reached out to whenever I needed a listening ear, sound advice, or a good kick in the butt. Up until his death, I could always count on him. He was there for me through every major life decision I've had to make; whether it was moving across country, getting married, getting pregnant, raising my kids, questioning my faith, or getting divorced. He was there and ALWAYS, ALWAYS put things in perspective for me. I miss him dearly, but I know he's smiling down on all of us!

---Michelle Felder-Jones
Associate Professor of Mathematics
Western Kentucky University

Coach Moultrie had an incredible impact on my life. He was much more than a track coach. Indeed, he was a life coach. It would be hard to nail down which one of his notorious sayings had the most impact on me, but the thing that impacted me most was how he handled disappointments. In my Sophomore year, I went to his office to tell him that I wouldn't be able to participate in the track program my Junior year because I was ineligible to run. I would need instead to focus on my academics and also get a job to pay for school.

Coach told us upon our acceptance onto the track team that he expected us to have a 3.0 or better every semester. I suffered from a 2 point something during my previous semester. He told me that my grades were unacceptable and that he would have to think it through as to whether or not to keep me on as a Track Bison. A few weeks into the cross-country season he called me into his office and told me that he had found some money to pay for my books and lodging, but that I would have to show him some real improvement that semester. I promised him that I would be a better track athlete – he told me that I needed to be a better man and that I needed to prove myself in the classroom and to my team mates. The faith that he put in me that day encouraged me to work harder than I ever had before in life. I had my best year in track that year and carried a 4.0 GPA that fall semester and a 3.7 overall for my Junior Year. I had an even better year in track and in the classroom during my Senior year and was named the captain of the Men's track team and became the student-athlete liaison for the Howard University administration. In typical fashion, Coach lauded my accomplishments at a team meeting, but told my teammates that there was nothing to cheer about – "Don't clap for Jomo, naw...he was only doing what he's supposed to do."

---Jomo Davis

My time as a Track Bison at Howard University, both as a freshman walk-on and later as team manager, was as intense as it was a treasure under the tutelage of our alchemist, Coach William P. Moultrie. He called me "East Point," because I hailed from East Point, GA. It was a nickname I was proud to hear him call me down to his last days.

At the time, I could not imagine how those cold and dark 5 a.m. cross-country track practices would pay off. Then, just a few years later, I met with more cold and dark mornings over my five-year orthopedic surgery residency just down Georgia Avenue at Howard University Hospital.

It was during those mornings that I heard Coach Moultrie's voice resounding in my head:
"Go to the elbows, East Point! Go to the elbows!" He was beckoning me to tap into the perseverance I had developed as a Track Bison. His words got me through many 36-hour days at the hospital.

"Suck it up! You betta suck it up!" This was Coach forewarning us that life would require just that from time to time. His simple words truly helped me in those wee hours of the morning when I wanted to collapse. I knew giving up wasn't an option.

Fast-forward to the day after I reached my goal of becoming a surgeon. I was walking along a busy street and spotted Coach walking up ahead. I caught up to him and we exchanged our latest news. At some point I shared with him that I was beyond frustrated with some of OUR people. Then he asked me:

"Hey Point! Have you read my new book?"

"What new book, Coach?"

"I titled it, L.N.A.F.!"

"L.N.A.F.? Coach, what does that stand for?" Now laughing and shaking my head. He then stomped his cowboy boots on the pavement, looked me square in the eyes and enunciated every word in his classic baritone voice:

"Leave N!$$@$ Alone ForEVA!"

All joking aside, the Lord knew how much I needed Coach in my life in preparation for my calling and to help me face life's challenges. We all did. For this, I remain forever grateful.

---Love you, Coach!
East Point
aka Dr. Bonnie Simpson Mason

When Brother Gerald Hector first approached me about recalling and sharing some of my memories of Coach William P. Moultrie, I must confess I was conflicted. Gerald had no way of knowing how dynamic and complicated my relationship with Coach was. What could I contribute, what could I say about a man so accomplished, so well loved, so instrumental in the lives of his student-athletes, that had not already been said?

While sitting down to write I settled on simply telling the truth. The truth of the matter is that Coach Moultrie was so many different things to so many different people. But the one common thread throughout all of the relationships I had the opportunity to observe, coupled with my personal experience, was that Coach Moultrie was always consistent. I, like many of his former athlete's, fondly remember the sayings and quips he commonly used to communicate his expectations. "You will run here or run away from here," "That Bison is going to Run," "The behind will do what the mind tells it to...move boot, be still boot!" All the while moving his boots to drive home the point that your body can push through the pain only if you will it to do so. I also recall the stern, disciplinary approach that he brought to the task of coaching.

My freshman class of 1987 was comprised of approximately 15 men and women who would become members of the Howard University Track Team. By the time of my graduation in 1991, nearly 90% of my track mates, with whom I had begun, had quit the track team. To be sure there were a number of factors that contributed to my teammates' decisions; the demands of class work, the desire to participate in other programs on campus, personal relationships, and more, but underlying them all was the demanding nature of our practices and the uncompromising expectation of our coach. But his techniques were the efficacy and importance of Coach Moultrie for many. Coach would see the potential in a person and would require, if not demand, that they do all that was humanly possible to reach their potential. It was true that you would either run there or run away from there as many chose to do. I did not quit during that time, not because I was special or even that I had run as hard as I could or adopted all of the philosophies of our coach. No, I didn't quit because of the singular most important lesson that I learned from Coach Moultrie: perseverance.

I appreciate Coach Moultrie for giving me an opportunity to attend Howard University. I appreciate all that he did in contributing to my evolution from boy to young man while at the University. I appreciate even the difficult lessons which he taught me about myself through raised voice before, during, and after practices and meets. But even more, I appreciate him for the one lesson that I employ most often, even some thirty-two years after first meeting Coach Moultrie, Don't Quit... Thanks Coach.

---Brian K. McDaniel, Esq.

Coach would declare: "It's a great day for a track meet," even when it was 34 degrees and raining. What that taught me was that it all boils down to a state of mind. Regardless of the weather, if you believe it's a great day for a track meet then you will perform like it's a great day for a track meet. It taught me to look beyond my current circumstances, and get the job done."

---Gita Bolt

Years after graduating from HU and retiring my track cleats, many of Coach William P. Moultrie's quotes still resonate with me. One quote in particular, "It's not about track it's about life" has a
very **particular meaning** to me to this day.

It's no secret that since I entered the HU program in 1991 at 17 years of age, I carried the belief that Coach Moultrie was very tough on me (we all probably felt that way at some point) and that I couldn't do anything right in his eyes. At times I felt that my accomplishments were diminished and my mistakes were magnified. I did not dislike or hate Coach Moultrie but at that time in my life it was hard for me to process the nature of our relationship outside of him being the coach and me being the student-athlete.

Fast forward to late May of 1998 and I had just recently completed my MBA program at the FW Olin Graduate School of Business at Babson College in Wellesley, MA. I needed an emotional recharge, so I decided to stop by Howard University and visit some of my professors at the School of Business. I bumped into Coach Moultrie in

194

front of Cooke Hall and we had our most meaningful conversation ever.

I discussed with him how challenging my MBA Program experience was and how living in Boston was difficult. That the environment and the interaction with the professors there was very different from that of my HU experience. In my two years in Boston I had learned a lot about myself, my strengths as well as my shortcomings. Two things helped to power me through this experience:

1. The promise that I made to my Mother to bring her home my MBA.

2. I was a Track Bison and that if I was mentally and physically able to persevere through four years as a student-athlete under Coach's tutelage, I could survive my MBA experience.

What I shared with Coach is that I'd started to grasp why he'd been so hard on me. I realized that his interactions with me were not from a place of disdain but rather from seeing a young undisciplined student-athlete and his desire to bring some structure to my life that frankly at that time, I was not used to. Essentially, he was helping me to build my mental toughness enabling me to meet life's challenges outside of the confines of the HU environment. Our five-minute conversation easily turned into an hour-long dialogue that I would never forget. I thanked Coach that day for being tough on me, sharpening my mental rigor, and ultimately seeing something in me that I perhaps had not seen in myself at the time. I apologized to him for any of my actions that were disrespectful to him. In classic Coach Moultrie fashion, he said "Son, it's not about track...it's about life!" To this day I am grateful to him for that conversation and all his life lessons and quotes that are guiding principles for me. Even now the "Mind continues to lead the behind."

---Carson Edwards Jr. MBA, CASE, CDMP
Global Account Executive
Marriott Global Sales, NA
Marriott International

"Coach Moultrie was not only a coach to me but my father as well. He gave so much to me, but besides his unwavering love, one of his many contributions to my life was an education at the esteemed Howard University. That experience was an incredible blessing that has helped shape me into the woman I am today, and for that, I will forever be grateful."

---Benita K. Nall
Actor/Writer

As you are aware, Coach William P. Moultrie was a one of a kind and an unforgettable character. What made this legendary Coach and Minister so unforgettable were the frequently crazy and somewhat insane things that would leave his mouth. As crazy and as thought provoking as much of those sayings were, much of what he said held a bit of truth and wisdom. His words have stuck with those of us who had the experience of seeing, hearing, and interacting with him.

It is very hard to pick just one nugget that Coach Moultrie shared that has provided some sort of illumination along my professional path, but one of the many that I have always employed is this one. "A smart rat has more than one hole." We would often hear Coach spout such pieces of wisdom, during one of his inordinate long after practice meetings. (everyone hoping he would wrap it up so we could get to the dining hall)...SMILE!

This particular quote was directed at the athletes who only wanted to run in one event. Since I was a walk-on and didn't mind running anything from the hurdles up to the 800 meters, he would point me out as an example to some of the scholarship athletes.
I have always had varied interests in life and in my professional pursuits. Being open to, and capable of successfully wearing multiple hats throughout my career has and continues to serve me well. In life, I always do my best "not to stink up the track."...SMILE! Coach Moultrie was indeed one of a kind.

---Bernard Oliver

"See boot, watch boot---the mind tells the behind what to do." "I don't need no names, just tell Henrietta you need your rest." "You not gonna make it." " It's a different world on the other side of Georgia Avenue." I can go on and on reminiscing on the quotes Coach Moultrie said to me. Those sayings helped define me as a man, a father, and a leader. I find myself utilizing those quotes too. My kids, friends, and employees have each heard me quote him at least once. Each time I reference one of his sayings, people look at me with a strange look and say "WHAT?" I just laugh to myself and ask them to think about it.

One of the biggest lessons I learned from Coach was not a quote. It was his wisdom. His discernment spoke volumes in my life and helped me develop into the leader I am today.

One day sitting in his office after the season had ended, he asked my opinion. This was not uncommon, but I was sure there was a lesson to follow.

"Bell do you think I should give this negro some money." Now see we had a few walk-ons in our program and coach was trying to decide if he should provide some scholarship money to some individuals based on their past year's performance. Naive me would always say "Yes Coach! They did a great job; I think they deserve it."

"Bell if I give him some money that negro is going to be no good."

"Huh?" Coach he worked hard. Who else do we have?"

As he typically did, he stood up, adjusted his britches (yes, he referred to his pants as britches all the time), looked me dead in my face, took his long black finger, poked me in the chest and said. "Bell once you reward some negros, they lose focus."

Over the last 20 plus years, I have hired, fired, and promoted many. I have interviewed so many individuals that I can now predict how they would be as an employee within the first two minutes. I still use the wisdom Coach shared with me all those years ago to help me make staffing decisions. The discernment is not only whether or not giving a person "the money" will cause them to lose focus. It implies that if you must ask for an opinion concerning your decision then you already know the answer :-)

> *"In the lips of him that hath discernment wisdom is found; But a rod is for the back of him that is void of understanding."* ---Proverbs 10:13 ASV.

Thanks Coach Moultrie, you have assisted me in ways I could not have imagined when I was going through the process. I am much better off because of it.

---Woodrow Shaun Bell

Okay, I remember Coach Moultrie pulling me to the side on more than one occasion and saying: "Jevon, Son you're only tired if you THINK you're tired. AND if you think you're tired, it is at that moment that it's time to go to work." I'm not sure if he ever said that to anyone else but he said it to me and I never forgot it. I apply that pretty much on a weekly basis. I audit clients Quality, Health and Safety and Environmental Management Systems all over the country. Needless to say, it can be stressful and very tiring, but I remember his words. That coupled with the fact that there are only a handful of people that look like me in this field so in some ways I am always in the spotlight. Like we all know "they" expect me to fail so giving up is unacceptable to me. Thanks Coach Moultrie.

---Jevon Williams

But I think, "We can run with anyone in the country!" definitely resonated with me while at Howard and afterwards. Those words also translate to - I can be anywhere and work with anyone in the country- I have always held my head high and had the confidence to be both the ONLY woman or black person in a leadership position or role. I have spent most of my career in IT - so both have been true. I remember going to a leadership training class a couple of years ago at Bank of America in Delaware- there were over 100 managers and directors in attendance. I was the only black face in the place. So again- "I can run with anyone in the country." Love Coach for all his priceless wisdom.

---Brenda Bailey Short

I work with exceptional high school students and one thing that Coach said to me has really helped me: "Stand up for what you believe." Every day I fight for these exceptional children to be given a chance to succeed. If that means advocating for them to have something added to their IEP, to help them become successful, or removing something from their IEP that has become a crutch, that's what I do...and I absolutely love it!

---Camille Hendrix

Listen to advice and accept instruction, that you may gain
wisdom in the future.
-Proverbs 19:20

I remember standing in the Miami International Airport awaiting my flight back to Washington, DC. Up walks Coach Moultrie who'd recognized me from my Howard University paraphernalia. I was from Jamaica and on a soccer scholarship to The Mecca. He chatted with us for a while, and told us how proud he was of us. That was the start of something I could never have imagined. From then on, Coach would invite us to his team meetings at the start of each academic year. His speech to the new recruits would start with, "I knew this gentleman was going to be a star. You want to know why? I relive that day often because of its serendipitous nature, but more importantly because there we were thinking that sports was our only option in pursuit of a dream much bigger than what we could comprehend at the time. Coach Moultrie had a way of seeing hidden talent and greatness in people before we could ever recognize it for ourselves.

---Bancroft Gordon
Vice President and Corporate Secretary
Marriott International

It's just short of 30 years since I first walked into the office of Howard University Athletic Director and Head Track & Field Coach William P. Moultrie. I was a first semester freshman, and other than the few newspaper clippings, track meet results, and the brief narrative he allowed me to share about my high school accolades as a hurdler, I was virtually unknown to him. I was at Howard University seeking an opportunity to join the track team as a walk-on student-athlete. After some concise vetting, Coach Moultrie told me "Son, sometimes in life the best you can hope for is a chance, it's up to you to make the most of it." Coach Moultrie went on to explain that he would "give me a shot at it," but I would be required to run cross-country in order to participate in the track & field season.

Four years later, as I began my senior year as a Howard University scholar student-athlete, Coach Moultrie gave me the honor of being named track team captain. He candidly shared with the team that, when I first arrived, I was "Just a guy, who did what I was supposed to when given a shot."

After graduating from college and working in corporate America for a few years, I decided to further my education by applying to law school. Given the profound respect I had for Coach Moultrie and the great influence he already had on my life, I humbly asked that he write a recommendation for my applications. He agreed, and he offered glowing words of support. When I went to pick up the recommendations, Coach Moultrie forecasted that I would "get a shot at attending law school," but again, I would have to make the most of the opportunity.

As Coach predicted, I was accepted at each law school to which I applied. I graduated from law school, passed the bar exam, and have been a civil litigation attorney for 20 years. I was the first African-American male named a law partner at my former law firm and I am currently senior in-house counsel for an insurance company.

During my private law firm practice, I was frequently called upon to interview and hire firm staff. On occasion, I found myself reflecting on the profound words (and actions) of one William P. Moultrie. I shared with some employee candidates the precious gift represented by being given a chance to prove yourself worthy of the opportunity before you. When warranted, I then extended that employment opportunity and provided support thereafter to maximize their chances of success.

THAT'S WHAT COACH MOULTRIE SHOWED ME...AND I HOPE THAT I'M DOING SOME THINGS TO PAY FORWARD THE BLESSING THAT HE WAS TO MY LIFE.

---Broderick Harrell